Praise for *Baby Dom/me/n*
A No-Frills Guide to Making Dc

"Baby Dom/me/mx Bootcamp covers a lot of useful ground for anyone entering sexualized labor—whether they want to dominate professionally or engage in other forms of sex work--and does so in a world where much of the information on marketing, running a business, and keeping ourselves safe has been obliterated by the effects of SESTA/FOSTA.
7 Days of Domination is the first time, to my knowledge, that this level of detailed information about being a pro Dom(etc.) has been collected and made available to complete beginners."

JESSICA STOYA, content creator and writer

"What a gift the BDBC is! So much dynamite advice conveyed with wit, wisdom, and a ton of heart, aimed at newbies, but with plenty of refresher info for the pro. If the wonderful world of Professional Domination is calling you, this is your trusty roadmap to guide you every step of the way."

LOLA DAVINA, former Professional Dominant, and author of the *Thriving in Sex Work* series

"Even if you are an experienced BDSM practitioner and know how to safely hogtie someone dressed as a priest, it doesn't mean you have the skills to safely charge your collard sub. This workbook is filled with everything you'd need to know before stepping into the world of professional domination. Eager clergy (and all other role players) await your service after gaining the newfound knowledge from this wonderful guide."

ERIC SPRANKLE, PSYD, professor of clinical psychology at Minnesota State University, Mankato

"The Baby Dom/me/mx Bootcamp Workbook is community wisdom and worker solidarity personified! The 7 Days crew extends their already ground-breaking project of online livestreams and education archives with this politically aware, business-savvy, thoroughly modern book. In a world where corporate tech interests and brutal criminalization make this industry ever more disorienting, 7 Days of Domination has managed to do the unthinkable: demystify the world's most mysterious profession."

TINA HORN, author of *Why Are People Into That? A Cultural Investigation of Kink*

"Lola Jean and Shayla Lange have transformed their popular weekend event into my favorite form, a workbook! Baby Dom/me/mx Bootcamp includes tips and questions to guide aspiring professionals through many of the important aspects of building a business thoughtfully. Baby Dom/me/mx Bootcamp will make a great addition to your kinky biz library!"

PRINCESS KALI, author of *Enough to Make You Blush* and *Authentic Kink*

TABLE OF CONTENTS

Chapter 1	**A Real Dom/me/mx Doesn't…**	4
Chapter 2	**New To SW**	5
Chapter 3	**House vs Independent**	12
Chapter 4	**Defining Your Own Success**	21
Chapter 5	**Understanding Your Power**	28
Chapter 6	**Common Newbie Mistakes**	34
Chapter 7	**Marketing Yourself**	43
Chapter 8	**Pre-Session Admin**	61
Chapter 9	**Asking For What You Want**	74
Chapter 10	**Negotiation**	83
Chapter 11	**First Time Sessions For Idiots**	91
Chapter 12	**When Sessions Go Wrong**	100
Chapter 13	**Personas, Style, Niches**	106
Chapter 14	**Social Media**	118
Chapter 15	**Culture and Etiquette**	126
Chapter 16	**Publicity**	132
Chapter 17	**Maintaining Client Relationships**	140
Chapter 18	**Cash Flow Post-Session**	151
Chapter 19	**Finances and Infrastructure**	159
	Case Studies	167
	Recommended Reading	172

WELCOME!

Congratulations! You are in, or want to enter into, the exciting career that is sex work. Maybe it is a temporary means of survival, a pitstop, or a final destination. No matter your reasons, we want to help you set yourself up for success– whatever that means to you– while maintaining safer practices and developing a risk profile.

Consider us the older siblings you never had, or the ones you wish you had. We're your fairy Dommemothers. Whether you are using this workbook as a guide alongside our in-person bootcamp or you're doing a self-study, we want to prepare you to figure out what works for you, as well as provide the kind of community that's necessary in this industry. You don't have to be alone if you don't want to.

This workbook is to help you guide your current practice or build a new one by supplying you with all the tools to create what works for you! Everyone's practice, offerings, risk profiles, and needs are going to be different.

This workbook operates in conjunction with our 7 Days of Domination online classes and talks. You not only gain information on a variety of topics and skills, you'll expose yourself to different Pro Dom/me/mx's styles, and perhaps become inspired to adopt a new practice. Take note of the recommended classes which accompany each section at the end of each chapter. PLUS, since you are (or are now) a sex worker (SWer), that means you get our SW discount. Check out the resource list in the back of this workbook for that information, along with other recommended readings and organizations.

This workbook isn't designed to be rushed through. Feel free to skip around and answer the questions with which you're most comfortable, then go through and have a long think about the remaining questions. More experienced workers will likely know much of this information, but it can feel overwhelming to someone who is brand new.

Never fear! Even the most veteran Dom/me/mx folks are continually learning, growing, and changing in their practice. Perhaps you've been doing in person work and want to move online, perhaps you've dabbled in online content but want to make more passive income, or venture down a different avenue of offerings. We get into the sex industry to make things work for us, not the other way around.

If you come across a word or phrase you don't know, that's okay. We all didn't know them at some point. We've tried to define some of the more commonly used terms and acronyms. The internet can be your friend for everything else. If you come across a word you don't identify with, feel free to cross it out and replace it with something you like better. This workbook is designed to be a guide to building your own practice and should be marked up, cut apart, and glued in to your heart's content.

CHAPTER 1

A REAL DOM/ME/MX DOESN'T...

A real Dom/me/mx doesn't....

Take their top off

Show their genitals

Service Top

Switch

Smile

Laugh

Sub in their personal life

Get out of bed for less than $500

Do full service

At some point, you're likely to hear one of these or something similar from someone in the industry. And it is flat out wrong.

This person is likely insecure about their own career or self, and projecting their ideas and values onto you.

A real Dom/me/mx can do whatever the fuck they want.

We didn't get into this industry because we like to follow rules. If anything, we want you to create new ones. Rules that feel authentic to you. Rules that spark joy. Rules that make you feel safe, celebrated, and however else you're looking to feel.

CHAPTER 2
NEW TO SW

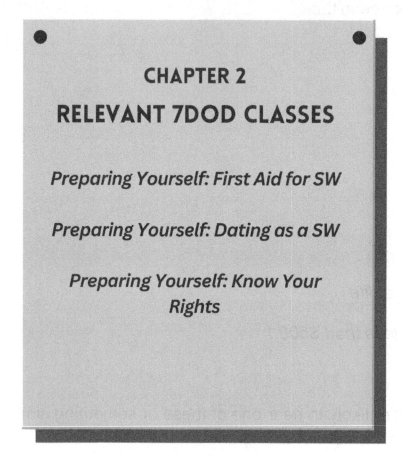

As a Pro Dominant, you are essentially a freelancer. This means no steady paychecks, no built in health insurance, and no paid time off. This can be scary for many coming from a corporate world or a fixed pay job entering a variable and volatile industry where planning can be tough. Building your career takes time. Building your clientele and community takes time.

All too often, we see folks come into the industry, make some quick cash, and then think "Oh man, I bet I would make way more than this if I could dedicate myself to it full time!" Beware of this mindset! In the industry this is referred to as "new girl/guy/them money," or NGM. NGM is the flutter of inquiries and bookings someone gets when they've first launched their career by putting up an ad on a new site or by being the most recent house hire. The idea is that since you're new, some clients will want to session with you because they want to try every local provider (aka "Dom/me/mx collectors"). Some will think you're too green to set boundaries, and book sessions where they try to test your limits. Some of them have burned so many bridges with so many providers that you're the only person who they could possibly session with. And some of them are lovely, wonderful humans who you will genuinely connect with on a kinky level. The latter will make up a very, very small part of your business in the beginning. Don't trust NGM, but enjoy it while it lasts.

Quitting your day job so you can devote more of your time to your Dominant business will not bring immediate results. If there are reasons other than being excited about your new career in BDSM that lead you to quit your job, *wonderful*. But if you *can* keep a foundation that allows this career to expand before you cut off your other resources, even another part time job, this can put less pressure on your timeline to success. Having an additional source of income makes you less likely to compromise your own boundaries in order to get the bag. We get it, you gotta do what you gotta do, but if you have the option, don't cut off your other legs until you're steady on these new ones.

Many workers, even the most established ones, still carry other jobs or gigs to diversify their income, even after they've reached their definition of success. This could account for seasonality, potential sickness, injury, or any other factor that would prevent someone from seeing clients.

SESTA/FOSTA

SESTA/FOSTA, or Stop Enabling Sex Traffickers Act and Fight Online Sex Trafficking Act respectively, is a series of laws handed down in February and March of 2018. These laws were supposedly intended to fight sex trafficking, as their names state, but ended up having the opposite effect.

Websites and ad directories promoting the sale of sexual services were previously protected under a set of laws from the Communications Decency Act of 1996– a set of laws that kept the owners of the individual platforms or the internet service providers themselves from being responsible for the words and ideas of its users.

SESTA/FOSTA specifically targeted sexual services for sale or trade. Under these new laws, anyone hosting content that "promotes prostitution" is at risk of being charged with a crime. Popular platforms that had long been hands-off when it came to buying and selling these services online, such as Craigslist or Backpage, were now broadly censoring anything even remotely sexual, in a CYA (cover your ass) maneuver that satisfied their legal teams.

This has more far reaching effects than just full service workers advertising online. All sexual services, legal or not, are being targeted. Social media platforms are quick to shadowban or suspend accounts thought to be associated with sex, even sex education. Banks can and will, without notice, shutter accounts receiving direct deposits from any venue that is considered "adult content," such as fansites or clip sites, even if the site provides no illegal services. The very writers of this book had a business bank account closed after only seven days, which is on brand but still annoying as shit. Even the perfectly legal porn websites have an ever-growing list of terms, phrases, and themes that are banned, based on what won't get them in trouble with the government or their credit card processors.

PRO TIP

If you want to do online work, consider opening up a new bank account (possibly at a different bank) for those direct deposits.

ON "SURVIVAL" WORK

Whorearchy; sometimes referred to as internalized whorephobia: the belief that some avenues of sex work are more degrading or demoralizing than others is extremely pervasive, even amongst sex workers themselves. Whether you're a Pro Dominant, a full service worker, a massage worker, a cam or porn performer, a stripper, etc., we are all under the red umbrella of "sex work," and all of us try to work at a level and in an area that feels good and sustainable for ourselves and our boundaries. Critics and enemies of sex workers will often paint a picture of every type of sex worker as a victim of abuse or of addiction, and claim that there is no such thing as consensual sex workers, and that we have no autonomy. Those people are wrong.

All labor under capitalism is "survival" labor, and sex work is no different. Some folks choose this life, and for some folks, economic or life circumstances mean that sex work is the only viable option for employment that fits all of their needs and wants. The high-gloss SWers who are out and proud about their houses, their handbags, their regulars, their cash flow, are just one facet of this business. There are also many workers who are living a more hand-to-mouth existence. *This is okay, and there is absolutely no shame in doing whatever you need to do to keep food on the table.* However, non-survival workers are often afforded more privilege than survival workers. For example, someone who works indoors might have more control over their security than someone who works outdoors or does dates in cars. Someone with even a small financial cushion may be able to say no to a booking that gives them a bad gut feeling. Not every worker has these privileges, and it is our goal in this book to get you to a level where you can set and enforce the boundaries that you choose, while still making the amount of money and/or having the schedule that you want.

If your goal is to get out of survival mode, your initial steps may be different than someone dipping a toe in as a side hustle. It's sometimes difficult to visualize long term success, or attempt to set up a sustainable foundation for your practice, if your current dreams are just to make this month's rent. We encourage you to not only list those immediate desires and needs, but also to dream bigger, past the horizon of your current goals. When you get to **CHAPTER 4: Defining Your Own Success**, start with the long term vision, and work backwards until you reach where you are now. Break down those goals into actionable items, and revisit/revise them as often as you'd like. You are not only capable, but powerful. You deserve more than to just keep food on the table. You deserve all of the good things that come at the top of the success ladder, regardless of where your position on it is at this moment.

COMMUNITY IS EVERYTHING

You're going to see a lot of mentions of community throughout this workbook. That is because it is vital in Pro Domination work. The day to day life of an independent Pro Dominant can often be lonely. There's no favorite coworkers on the same shift, no team meetings, no senior staff to answer newer folks' questions. Independent workers have to build their communities and network of other pros on their own. We cannot thrive without it.

Community can provide friendship and camaraderie, which is lovely, but it also provides safety, business, and legitimacy, which is crucial. You will need community to vet and screen clients, other workers, events, and even brands, for red or green flags. We are the only ones who keep us safe.

Community can directly contribute to your income: maybe a fellow pro invites you in on a double session, refers a client to you, or suggests you to their own network by reposting your tour announcement or social media posts. Other workers can be a source of education through institutional knowledge and skill-shares.

Community doesn't have to be a group of individuals with five or ten+ years of experience. A group of "littermates" (i.e. friends you make who start in the industry around the same time as you) can be one of your best assets, and an asset that will only get more powerful as time goes on.

You will get out of community what you put into it.

Look at local advertising websites to see who's around you. Follow them on social media. This can be a helpful baseline to see what's going on in your neck of the woods.

COMMUNITY OVER COMPETITION

It's easy to see so many dom/me/mxs and compare yourself to them, feel like the market is oversaturated, or that there's no room for you. This is a myth. There are lots of perverts in the world, enough to keep everyone's practice thriving and food on everyone's table. Your fellow pros aren't your enemy, they are a lifeline. Your friends and fellows can inspire you, teach you, offer support, and keep you safe. They will understand this job better than your civilian besties/partners/family ever could. They are not, and will never be, your competition. The idea of competition is a direct threat to community building, and we cannot reiterate that no other Dominant is your direct competition, as much as the internet makes it feel that way.

This is an unregulated industry, which has its benefits and drawbacks. On one hand, there's less gatekeeping on industry entry, and you don't need a certificate or degree to become successful in this industry. On the other hand, anyone can wedge their way into this world. Some Dominants have different risk profiles and practices, and may burnout quickly because of this. This is why community and reputation is paramount. There is reputation amongst colleagues and reputation amongst clients. One is not indicative of the other.

IN SUMMARY

1. You're new to this, even if you've been domming in your personal life you're new to this career. Don't be so hard on yourself.
2. You are capable of much more than you think. Set realistic expectations and continue to surpass them.
3. Be mindful online.
4. Build community like your life depends on it, because it does.

CHAPTER 2: NEW TO SW

Think about what you want to get out out of this career and what you have to gain.

WHY DO I WANT TO BE A SEX WORKER?

WHAT DO I WANT TO GAIN FROM THIS INDUSTRY?

HOMEWORK

List three current or former sex workers you admire.

CHAPTER 3
HOUSE VS INDEPENDENT

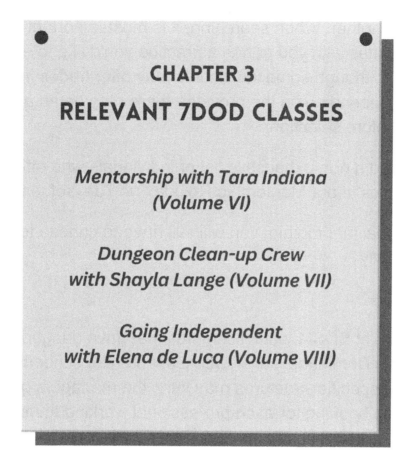

WHERE TO START

There are generally three routes to learning and training in this industry: **House, Independent, and Mentorship.**

Whichever you choose mostly depends on your learning style, how much you feel you need to learn/experience and which will make you the most comfortable. None of these options are a "better" route than the other or will fast track you to success over another.

MENTORSHIP

A mentorship is one-on-one training with an established Pro Dominant. They can answer your questions, teach you physical skills as well as the "soft skills" that are necessary in this industry. They can potentially introduce you to some of their network too. Not all Pros offer mentorships, and those who do have vastly different programs from one another. When searching, it is most important that you pick a Dominant who resonates with you or has a practice you'd like to emulate. Most mentorships are paid, though some individuals may offer trades in exchange for their labor of mentoring. Depending on the provider, there may be an application and screening process before selection.

We have accumulated a non-exhaustive list of individuals who offer both in person and virtual mentorships in our Mentorship Rolodex on 7daysofdomination.com

Even if you do a formal mentorship, you will still have to choose to work either in a house or independently.

HOUSES

Houses are "houses" of BDSM: establishments that have dungeon/session rooms, contract a staff of Pro Dominants/subs/switches, and take scheduled and walk-in clients. Though their specific structures may vary, the managers generally handle all of the advertising and booking for each professional working there, so the pro only has to show up for their shifts and see the assigned clients.

Independent Dominants/subs/switches are workers who are completely independent. They control their own advertising, book their own clients, arrange session space, and maintain a collection of their own gear.

Both have their benefits and disadvantages, and both can be done very well... or very poorly.

Houses are infamous for paying low rates, having minimal/no screening of clients, and sometimes having overbearing managers or owners who, at best, violate labor laws, and at worse, book unsafe or abusive clientele. House workers are often classified as "independent contractors." This means the workers have little/no labor protections, and little recourse if a session goes horribly wrong. Houses are also relatively uncommon outside of major metropolitan areas, so finding one in your area may be difficult.

Houses do have some benefits, and there's a reason why many successful independent Dominants started in one. Houses provide a plug-and-play option for workers who are just starting out, workers who might not want to be full time, or workers who want a clearer work/life balance. This is where you can try on different hats, both literally and metaphorically, to figure out what your style of Domination is. A house provides a facility in which to meet clients and the equipment to use with said clients. The house handles all of the advertising and booking. The workers who've been there longer can share their collective memory of knowledge and history with those just starting. It's a great place to ask questions and experience sessions and styles that are different from your own. It's a place where someone just starting out can feel like it's okay to make mistakes, ask questions, and experiment until they find their groove. On the flip side, the quality and reputability of which house dominants are training and/or mentoring you can be luck of the draw.

> *You didn't just share information about sessions, but support. When you worked in house, if you had a bad session, when you came out…there was a roomful of women that understood. Because even if you have straight friends that are compassionate, they're not really going to understand what a bad session is.*

FROM MENTORSHIP WITH TARA INDIANA (VOLUME VI)

Generally speaking, the clients who frequent houses are going to be much different than the ones who seek out independents, as many are chasing a new flavor of the week, rather than trying to build a relationship with a trusted professional.

Sometimes, the house model can feel catty or competitive. Always remember your fellow workers are your colleagues and collaborators, not your competition. There are enough perverts in the world to feed everyone, remember?

When choosing a house, look out for some common red flags:
Price transparency: do you know how much the client paid for the session vs what your cut is?

Is the owner or manager asking to "sample the wares" or asking you to do an unpaid "audition" session with the client?

Do you feel as if you can say "no" before or during a session?

PRO TIP

Some houses ask you to start as a pro-submissive or switch before they market you as a Pro-Dominant. Consider what you can learn from this experience and practice setting boundaries early and often if you choose to go this route.

INDEPENDENTLY INDEPENDENT

If you've chosen to go independent off the bat, but don't have experience in BDSM or sex work, where do you start? Luckily, you have this book, which is a great first step. No matter which route you take, it should always be bolstered by continuing education by well established Dom/me/mxs. This education can vary in price. Vet your educators before committing large sums of money to more extensive programs.

Independent workers will find they have more control over their offerings both in person and online; this might include outcalls, custom clips, or niches that don't fly in a particular house. Independent workers can always turn down clients they don't like, or ones that give them the heebie jeebies. Indie folks can screen using whatever method they prefer, and set their tributes at a rate that feels good for them, all without having to give a dime to anyone else. Indie folks also have no required shifts or restrictions on when or where they work.

The downsides of indie work is now you're responsible for EVERYTHING. Session space can be hard to find and/or costly. Equipment is expensive. Advertising is getting harder by the day, and the sheer amount of admin work can weigh down the joy of the physical work. This type of work has a tendency to feel isolating with the lack of built-in community. Getting social proof can be difficult.

Most Dom/me/mxs who start in a house gain enough confidence and experience to eventually make the decision to go indie, but not everyone wants or needs the independent life. Both options are valid, and everyone's practice has different needs and desires. It's up to you to determine what feels good for you.

> **IN SUMMARY**
>
> Houses, mentorships and independent work all have their pros and cons. None of them are the "one true way," but there is something to be learned from all three.

CHAPTER 3: HOUSE VS INDEPENDENT

Think about your work structure as you fill this out at your leisure.

WHAT ARE MY DEALBREAKERS FOR CHOOSING A HOUSE?

WHAT IS MY PREFERRED LEARNING STYLE?

WHAT PERSONAL NEEDS CAN EACH MODEL FULFILL FOR ME?

| WHAT CLASSES OR WORKSPACES EXIST IN MY LOCAL AREA? | WHAT ARE THE MAIN RISKS I RUN BEING INDEPENDENT? |

HOW WILL I BUILD KNOWLEDGE, COMMUNITY, AND EXPOSURE WITHOUT A HOUSE MODEL?

CHAPTER 3: MENTORSHIP

If you're interested in going down the mentorship route, answer these questions first.

WHAT QUALITIES ARE IMPORTANT TO ME IN A MENTOR?

WHAT AM I HOPING TO LEARN THAT I CAN'T GET FROM A HOUSE MODEL?

WHAT TYPE OF TIME OR MONETARY COMMITMENT AM I REALISTICALLY ABLE AND WILLING TO PUT INTO A MENTORSHIP?

HOW WILL I KNOW WHEN I AM READY TO GO INDEPENDENT?

HOMEWORK

Find the closest house location to you.

List two providers that you know offer mentorships.

CHAPTER 4
DEFINING YOUR OWN SUCCESS

> **CHAPTER 4**
> **RELEVANT 7DOD CLASSES**
>
> *Career Longevity & Professionalism with Michelle Lacy (Volume III)*
>
> *What I've Learned from 20+ yrs of Personal & Pro BDSM with Simone Justice (Volume VI)*
>
> *Avoiding Burnout with Lola Davina (Volume XIII)*

The number of followers you have, sessions per week you book, or even how much money you make is not the universal definition of success. Many who hit big number goals quickly may also burn out and leave the industry... which is great if that's what they want, but that is also why defining your own success is so important. Keep your eyes on your own prize and do not constantly compare yourself to others.

How you define success will change year to year, so **it's a good idea to revisit this section of the workbook as often as you need.**

Your stamina and patience will likely shift over time. Take advantage of when you have a lot of hustle in you, but also be wary of burnout!

What does success look like to you? Is it the amount of sessions you take a week? The price per session? Is it a steady income? Owning a dungeon? Being able to pick and choose your clients? The ability to say no to sessions you don't want to do? To retire?

WHAT IT TAKES TO BECOME A LEGEND

What comes to your mind when you think of a Pro Dom/me/mx legend? Is it endless glossy photoshoots showing off their extensive leather, latex, and Louboutin wardrobe? Is it a multi-story dungeon, filled with an impossible amount of gear? Is it a clipstore with 20 years of content, showcasing a stable of loyal submissives serving their every need?

It may surprise you that there are individuals who have not only survived, but thrived, for 20, 40, even 50+ years in this industry. All of those legends have much in common– and it's not gizmos and gadgets a'plenty. Every Pro-BDSM legend has gotten where they are through consistent and intentional hard work. They maintain this seemingly endless stamina by building a system, creating professional boundaries, and taking breaks.

Keep this in mind as you build the foundations of your practice and beyond. Success doesn't happen overnight, and it doesn't always last. If longevity in the business is your goal, look to the careers of the Dom/me/mx-cestors that came before us.

TARA INDIANA'S KEYS TO LONGEVITY IN THE BUSINESS

Take Breaks: We don't get the luxury of being able to take paid leave like our capitalist counterparts. A break could mean getting a vanilla job for 3 months out of the year so you can reboot and refresh. It could mean you keep your weekends sacred and work-free. No matter what the plan is, taking breaks keeps the burnout at bay.

Diversify your income: Multiple streams of income can help in wake of an emergency. Whether you break your tailbone, a global pandemic prevents you from taking in-person sessions, or all clip stores cease business overnight, you want something (or several somethings) to fall back on that will keep you afloat.

Have friends and/or activities not in SW: We get it, whores make some of the best company, and this doesn't mean don't hang out with fellow Pros. But it is important to keep yourself involved in activities or people you enjoy outside of sex work, to ensure all of your socializing doesn't become talking shop. Ground yourself by investing in "civilian" hobbies and friendships.

Be Empathetic & Apathetic: It's important to hold space for our clients, our fellow workers, and the kink community at large, but we don't have to let it consume us. Every one of us has things we care about (and things we don't care about at all). Lean into those, set boundaries that protect your energy, and let go of the things that genuinely don't matter.

Create good work boundaries: In those first few years, everything is new and shiny and exciting. It may feel like every client is a pokemon and you gotta catch (and keep) 'em all! But setting hard boundaries around your time, energy, and physical space in a work context helps keep clients, colleagues, and yourself in the right places.

Don't be a Diva: You want people to want to work with you. Holding onto or being the drama is as painful for others as it is ourselves. Be professional, courteous, and show the same respect for others as you would want shown to you.

Have a non-SW side hustle: If you are truly burnt out from sex work but don't have a financial safety net, the last thing you may want to do is more sex work to make ends meet. Even if the side hustle isn't super active, having a "way out" if needed may prevent you from making choices or seeing clients you otherwise wouldn't.

Imposter syndrome is the idea or belief that we don't actually know what we're doing, and that one day someone will expose us for the fake that we are. This is a common feeling, especially amongst the self-employed. There's no "Dominant degree" we can point to on the wall, no awards or promotions we can strive for. It's easy to fall deep into imposter syndrome, to get discouraged, and even decide to quit because we don't feel like our skills are up to snuff, or we're not as far along in our journey as we wish we were.

On the other hand, imposter syndrome can sometimes be helpful; it can push us to keep learning, to sharpen our skills, to form meaningful connections with others in the industry. Getting better at what you do is the only way to feel more comfortable in your own practice as a pro.

CHAPTER 4: DEFINING YOUR OWN SUCCESS

Think about what success means to you
as you answer these questions.

WHAT DOES SUCCESS LOOK LIKE TO ME?

WHAT DO I NEED TO MOVE OUT OF SURVIVAL SW?

IN 5 YEARS

IN 10 YEARS

WHAT ACTIVATES MY IMPOSTER SYNDROME?	**WHAT STEPS AM I TAKING TO DEAL WITH MY IMPOSTER SYNDROME?**
HOW WILL I KNOW WHEN I'VE REACHED "SUCCESS?"	**WHAT IS MY TIMELINE FOR REEVALUATING MY GOALS?**

HOMEWORK

Draw, paint, or collage a vision board of your long term success. Include ideas, feelings, and physical items.

CHAPTER 5
UNDERSTANDING YOUR POWER

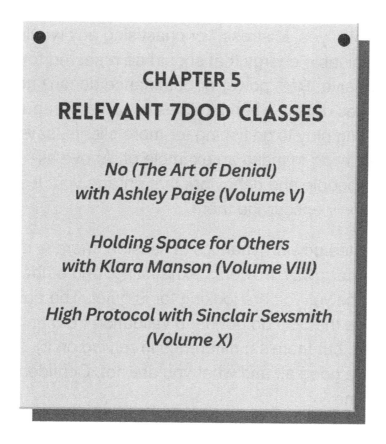

Being a Dominatrix is not your one-stop-shop for becoming empowered or exploring your sexual identity. BDBC is first and foremost a business program, because being a Dominatrix is a business. Like any job, you will learn more about yourself, especially as you gain more experience in handling different clients and situations. When you progress and experience more in your job, you may gain confidence in what you do. That confidence often translates to other aspects of your life, which is pretty rad.

Before any negotiated power dynamics take place, there will always be the foundational power dynamic of provider and client. This is not where you will begin your BDSM power dynamics (don't let them get this shit for free) but it *is* where your professionalism starts. You still need to hook the client. That doesn't mean you have to grovel and beg for business. It means that they are not an official client until money is exchanged. That being said, negotiation and aftercare time also fall into professionalism. Meaning: you do not have to be "in character" or operating within additional power dynamics in these moments.

This is where a lot of misused appropriations of power happen. It may be tempting to flex your power, status, or dominance, especially on a potential walking ATM who infiltrates your inbox with "yes, Mistress," or chastising any would-be-submissive who doesn't. This is your valuable energy that should be reserved for a session. It also can read as green or naive. Real power or dominance doesn't need to be regularly flexed publicly (that goes double when it relates to your colleagues). Unless you're using this as a marketing ploy to go fishing for more clients, save the "how dare they" for those you are truly trying to make an example of. Above all– if you can afford to– try not to engage with people and behaviors that enrage you. It's not worth your energy, and will likely only encourage them.

Outside of any negotiated power dynamics in session, there is no need to exert your power *or* take their power away. Power is exhausting, and embodying it at all times is rarely necessary. The power you are looking for is quiet. The power you desire is confidence. Confidence that you do not need validation from anyone else (validation can certainly feel good, but there's a difference in *relying* on it). Confidence that you can name what you are good at, and what you are not. Confidence that you do not need anything or anyone.

PRO TIP

Let's say a client contacts you saying they love impact play, stinky feet, and rope suspension. You might not know the first thing about rope, but want to take the session. It doesn't make you any less powerful to say "I'm newer to rope - but I love <insert other bondage skill in here.>" Alternatively - instead of *faking it till you make it* and potentially injuring the client, how about suggesting a double with another provider who does have experience with this kink?

Yes, some clients will quickly and easily hand you their submission, along with an instruction manual on what to do to them. Others may need time to build trust and communication. You may also need time to build trust and communication for more demanding sessions. This can be achieved through professionalism, email exchanges, and/or paid phone calls on niteflirt.

Think of the civilian's stereotypical idea of a Dominatrix. They are terrifying, mean, sometimes yelling, and take no bullshit. Isn't living up to an expectation exhausting? You do not have to embody someone else's– or even your own– idea of what a Dominatrix is at all times.

How you handle yourself and navigate relationships with colleagues is completely different from that of your clients or potential clients. You do not have an agreed power dynamic with other providers. Most are not concerned with how many clients you have, how successful you are, what nice thing someone bought off your wishlist etc... For facilitating relationships with other workers, check out **CHAPTER 15: Culture and Etiquette.**

Power dynamics are a funny thing. Who holds the power, and how can we turn that on its head? You hold inherent power here, just by being the Pro Dominant that the client seeks out. When you are contacted, the client is asking for something: your time, your attention, your smelly socks, etc. You have the power to grant or deny their wish. Being professional from the get-go is important here; the clients aren't mind readers, and you should gently correct them when and where they go wrong. You don't need to "take" their power from them, and you don't have to "prove" you're the dominant. Think about the worst manager you've ever had. Did they set you up for success in your job? Did they organize and enable their employees to always know what the corporate policies were, and enforce them to the best of their ability? Probably not.

You're the manager here. Actually... you're the CEO of the whole damn company. One of the most important parts of your job is to let your team members (aka clients) know clearly and concisely what their roles are, and how they are to behave. This means not yelling at them about using the wrong honorific in a first email. This means learning what they are good at, and harnessing that ability to work for you.

IN SUMMARY

One does not need to "prove" their power. It comes from the confidence that you can both handle and survive regardless of your needs and wants being met.

CHAPTER 5: UNDERSTANDING YOUR POWER

What does power mean to you? Examine your thoughts on this complex topic through these questions.

WHAT DOES POWER MEAN TO ME?	WHAT MAKES ME FEEL CONFIDENT?

WHERE DO I FEEL THE MOST POWER ON A DAILY BASIS?	HOW WILL I CHANNEL MY CONFIDENCE INTO OTHER AREAS OF MY LIFE AND PRACTICE?

HOMEWORK

Do your best fly-on-the-wall and observe ways that power shows up around you.

What does this power look like?

How does it feel?

Do certain types of power feel 'better' than others?

CHAPTER 6
COMMON NEWBIE MISTAKES

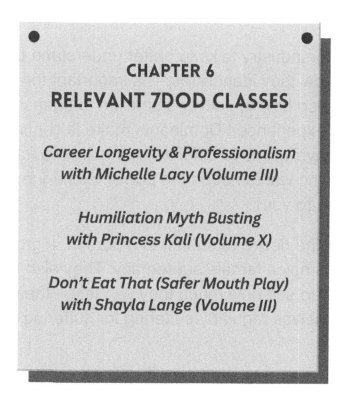

CHAPTER 6
RELEVANT 7DOD CLASSES

Career Longevity & Professionalism with Michelle Lacy (Volume III)

Humiliation Myth Busting with Princess Kali (Volume X)

Don't Eat That (Safer Mouth Play) with Shayla Lange (Volume III)

Ahhh, newbie mistakes. We've all made them. Sometimes we *still* make them. Did you tell your client to drop to his knees and worship your boots, and instead he stuck out his tongue and said "make me"? Did you improperly warm up a bottom and leave marks that will last much longer than anticipated? Did CashApp accidentally reveal your full government name? It's a LOT to learn, and no one does it perfectly.

> We're not in an instant industry. We need to develop a reputation for ourselves with good reviews, submissives online singing our praises from good sessions, and videos that they can watch just to see that we really are who we say we are.

FROM CAREER LONGEVITY & PROFESSIONALISM
WITH MICHELLE LACY (VOLUME III)

There are far too many newbie mistakes to list here. Every single Dominant on the face of the earth has a story about when they made a newbie mistake. While there is nothing wrong with learning from mistakes, it also shouldn't be your default method of learning!

SUBMISSIVE VS FETISHIST

This language is used for industry folks to better understand the client's mindset– what the client wants, how they identify, etc.– is important for not only determining if this is a fit for you, but also how to deliver a session to quench both of your thirsts. A common mistake even experienced Dominants make is conflating fetishists with submissives. A submissive will have different needs than a fetishist. A submissive identifies as someone who wants/needs the power exchange to happen. They *must* submit (and normally it's to you).

Submissives may have the desire to submit to a person, a group, or an identity– for example, those who champion female supremacy. They also may embody the desire to submit to themselves to see how much they can take– the classic man vs nature. A client who finds themselves regularly suffering for suffering's sake may find this appealing.

A fetishist *may* get off on power exchange, but outside of a scene, it's generally not a motivating factor. This may be someone who's enthusiastic about one specific thing, such as latex, pegging, etc. Taboo fetishists may not be specific about their wants or needs; just the fact that they're sneaking around in the dark to do depraved and perverted things is enough.

There are other archetypes and sub-archetypes (pun intended) but these are the big two– and the two that newbies often get wrong.

Ask a submissive what their ideal fantasy is, and they might say "Whatever you want, Mistress." Telling a fetishist to lick your boots or do your laundry might be met with bored eyerolls or outright refusals. Understanding the difference between the two will help guide your interactions with a client from the moment of meeting, throughout your time together and beyond.

Because society has utterly confused men about how their desires are not related to their masculinity (for more: see *Boys & Sex* on the recommended reading list) many clients may tell you they are submissive, but once you get behind the dungeon doors you seem more like bros having fun putting things into eachothers' orifices. This is because many people confuse bottoming with being submissive. They think if they enjoy certain activities, they must be submissive…right?

Wrong. You'll get better at sniffing out a fetishist versus a submissive over time. Perhaps you'll even develop a preference for one over the other.

PRO TIP

Some older clients or those who cut their client teeth in houses in the 80's, 90's or early 00's may refer to themselves as "slave" regardless of their hierarchical identifications or desires. Many houses/old guard pros used "Mistress/slave" in place of "Provider/client". This has largely fallen out of fashion, in no small part because of the connotations of the word slave, but also because not every provider is a "Mistress" and not every client can be summed up in an easy word like slave or submissive.

NOT COMMUNICATING EXPECTATIONS CLEARLY

Another common newbie mistake is letting someone off the hook for bad or gross behavior. What kind of behavior? We're glad you asked...

EXAMPLE 1

A client may not have cleaned out properly before anal play, and you find that out mid-session. It's your first session together and you want them to come back for a second, so you couldn't possibly risk hurting their feelings....right? In the meantime, you suffer. The session ends and you walk back to the dressing room smelling like literal shit. You wonder if this is your life.

EXAMPLE 2

A client waltzes into your session and asks to worship your body. You have a lot of experience with foot worship, so you're fine with this. The client starts licking a little further up in an aggressive way and you freeze. You try to take control of the situation.

"How do my sweaty feet taste?" You ask. He does not respond. He is fixated on the licking, eyes glazed over. You stand there, rolling your eyes while a man drools on your ankles for half an hour, just waiting out the clock. You leave the session disassociated. You wonder if this is your life.

Both of these are real situations that have happened to one of the authors of this book. These situations are because this person didn't know how to set boundaries, communicate expectations, and was fearful of the wrong thing (losing a client or a session). They could have stated very clearly up front: "clean out before you arrive" or "you will not be permitted to slobber on me." They could have also gently guided verbally during the session: "you're a bit messy, why don't we change gears," "slobbering on me isn't my ideal form of worship, you should massage instead," or by reacting physically to the event. Client #1 gets an enema as a humiliating end to a session. Client #2 could have been bound and gagged, forced instead to keep it together while our Domme teased him with said delicious feet.

PRO TIP

Someone get handsy in a session and you don't like it? Put socks over their hands and cuff their wrists together. For a humiliating twist: choose socks that have a silly print.

PLAYING ABOVE YOUR SKILL LEVEL

Before the internet, the way one learned BDSM technique was "see one, do one, teach one." You saw someone throwing floggers at a party, and now you want to do this. Maybe you saw a performance involving blood and you thought "that's pretty simple." Or you took a rope class and now want to tie everyone up, all the time.

These are all perfectly wonderful things. But they can sometimes play out poorly. A furiously thrown flogger wraps around the body, leaving marks in conspicuous places. A needle improperly placed leads to accidental sticking, and suddenly you're fluid bonded with a stranger. The rope tension is all wrong, so it slides around and pinches a nerve. There's some truth to practice makes perfect– you don't have to be perfect, but you do have to practice. **Risk-Aware Consensual Kink** (RACK) dictates that both you and your bottom know your own bodies and your own skill levels (see **CHAPTER 12: When Sessions Go Wrong**). If your bottom knows that you like rope, and you want to practice on/with them, that's perfectly fine. But claiming you're a shibari expert when you're not is a great way to not only hurt someone's body, but also your reputation. There is absolutely no shame in playing at a beginner's skill level; not everyone will ask for (or even want) a 10-foot bullwhip session or a heavy medical scene. There's plenty of people who desire play at every level, and plenty of clients who will revel in being your test dummy. The trick is to figure out what you *do* know well, communicate that to your clients, and walk in confident, knowing that everything you're about to do, you're going to do *extremely well.*

PRO TIP

Some professionals offer discounted "practice sessions" where they practice a skill on a client's body. Make it clear that you'll be wearing whatever you want, and that you'll only be practicing whatever that specific skill is. This can be a great way to perfect your technique, and maybe even attract someone who's experienced at this type of play.

This carries into parties and play spaces. It's important to learn the rules of a space/venue/party before attending. Some spots are free-for-alls and some have specific rules about play and cleanup. At parties, greeting someone you just met with "you will address me only as Goddess X, and never speak unless spoken to" is generally not going to fly.

IN SUMMARY

1. Not everyone is submissive.
2. Ask for what you want, tell them what you don't.
3. Play with what you know, practice what you don't.

CHAPTER 6: COMMON NEWBIE MISTAKES

Mistakes, they're inevitable.
Plan for the unexpected to minimize the damage.

WHAT SKILLS DO I KNOW I AM GOOD AT?

WHAT SKILLS DO I WANT TO LEARN? HOW DO I PLAN TO LEARN THEM?

HOW WILL I KNOW WHEN I AM READY TO BRING A NEWLY LEARNED SKILL INTO MY PRACTICE?

THREE BOUNDARIES I WILL COMMUNICATE UPFRONT

HOW WILL I ENFORCE THOSE BOUNDARIES WITH CLIENTS?

WHAT QUESTIONS WILL I ASK MY CLIENTS TO UNDERSTAND IF THEY ARE A SUBMISSIVE VERSUS A FETISHIST?

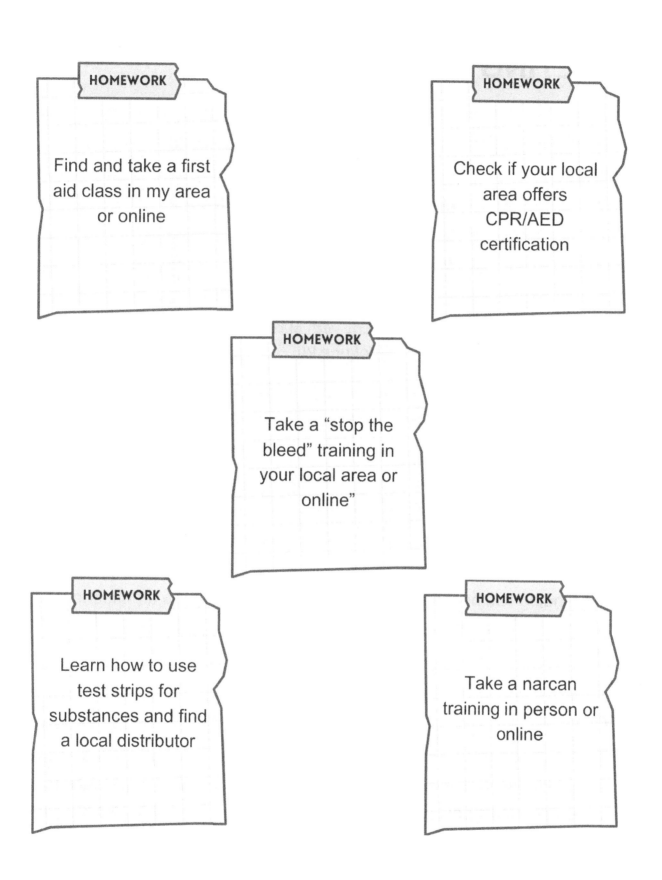

CHAPTER 7
MARKETING YOURSELF

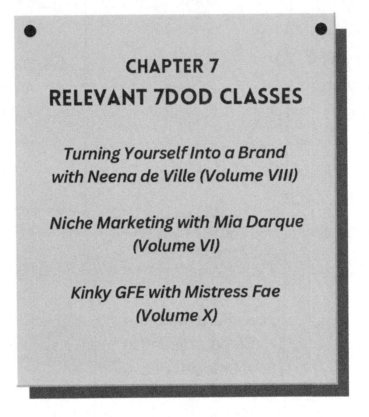

**CHAPTER 7
RELEVANT 7DOD CLASSES**

*Turning Yourself Into a Brand
with Neena de Ville (Volume VIII)*

*Niche Marketing with Mia Darque
(Volume VI)*

*Kinky GFE with Mistress Fae
(Volume X)*

BRANDING

The word branding can be intimidating. Are you supposed to be a household soft drink? Do you need a tagline? A logo? While all of these things are lovely and fun, they are not necessary to have a strong brand. Sometimes you need to fuck around before you find out.

Maybe you've heard of archetypes and personas and are quick to pinpoint and figure out your own. You do not need a fully fleshed out persona when starting. Often, this is something you will hone in on over time; the more you play, the more you get to know your Dominant personality. Your brand is encased in the way you talk, look, and engage. This works best when it feels natural to you. Try not to feel pressured to be like that Dom/me/mx you saw on the internet, and instead figure out who you are and what feels natural to your current state. TLDR: you don't have to appear "upscale" to make bank. If you try to emulate something you're not, it will be palpable. You want to create a brand and persona that is *fun* to maintain.

Think of branding as storytelling. What are you trying to say with every piece of media, text, and content you put out there? One of the most important stories you can tell is with your imagery. Anyone can look hot while they stare down the lens of a camera, but what are you trying to say with your photos? Are you just holding the prop or are you using it to engage with the camera, POV-style? Can the viewer insert themselves into someone's shoes in the photo? Are you face in or face out? How can you make the setting, the props, and the overall vibe work for your storytelling? If you struggle with giving face, remember that it is a static image. You can scream, laugh, or have a whole ass conversation to get your point across on camera.

Whether it's a caption, a blog post, a photo, ask yourself who the media is intended for: the client or other workers? It is for other workers, but something a client may enjoy anyway? Clients and potential clients typically want to consume as much content as possible to get to know you. This doesn't necessarily mean they will pay for that content, but it does mean they probably read every tweet you sent in the last year and every. single. photo. in your gallery. You don't always need to be talking directly to them to get them listening. This strategy may be different based on the platform as well.

Revisit your brand every few years as you grow and get to know yourself and your practice. The longer you work, the easier it becomes to hone in on your brand and what sets you apart from others. Hint: it's going to be much more than your look alone.

DO try on multiple hats. Ask any Dominant who has been in the space multiple years if they're doing what they were interested in when they started. This doesn't mean you have to compromise your personal boundaries, but know that your interests and your persona may change!

DON'T invest in fancy tools too early. Many thought they'd be doing more flogging in this industry only to find that leather baddie collecting dust on the shelf. A good rule of thumb is to invest in a more expensive tool or item once the cheaper version breaks, because then you know you're actually using it.

DO choose items that are easy to clean. You have no idea how thankful you'll be that you bought that neoprene strap-on harness and not the leather one.

DON'T focus too much on the wardrobe. Unless it is the fetish itself, like latex or nylons, there isn't as much need to have an extensive collection. The heels you see in Dominants' photoshoots aren't always worn in sessions. Any pro that's been in the industry long enough has transitioned their session wardrobe into something that is comfortable for them. Some clients even like it when you wear the same thing each session, especially if it plays into their fantasy.

PRO TIP

Someone who wants to project a "strict disciplinarian" image might not crack jokes about very silly things that happened in scene. Someone who embraces a more casual "bully next door" might not post images and text about high protocol.

WHAT'S IN A NAME?

You may have a name picked out before you even opened this book. Something you've loved. A name that rang true and so perfectly encapsulated you and your personality...only to find out that there's already a Dom/me/mx with the same name or the same honorific. Maybe even one in your city already. Perhaps you're the opposite— totally stumped as to what to call yourself, any idea you've had was taken, or just nothing feels right.

The good news is, it doesn't matter. The only thing that matters is that it's 1. easy to spell, 2. attached to an honorific you identify with, and 3. not taken by someone already established in your community.

Let's take, for example, the most popular baby name of 2020: Olivia. A cursory search for "Mistress Olivia" on the major platforms brings up hundreds, possibly even thousands of accounts. You may be the only Olivia in your town, but on the internet, it's easy to get lost in the worldwide shuffle.

So what now? Are you relegated to obscure or outdated names like Gertrude or Wilhelmina (as of printing, no current listings for "Mistress Wilhelmina")? The answer is no. You don't have to be completely unique, you just have to be unique enough to not get lost. Honorifics or adding a last name can do a lot of heavy lifting here. Getting extremely niche or stylized with your branding can also help set you apart if you already have an established name for yourself.

Ask yourself:

What are names that speak to me?
What honorifics speak to me?
Are there any established professionals out there that I might get confused with?

HONORIFICS

An honorific is a title that denotes power and standing, the most common ones being "Mistress/Mistrix/Master" or "Goddess/Goddex/God," but there are endless titles out there that could encapsulate your persona or style.

Why have an honorific?

Having a title creates an automatic power dynamic. You are the Deity, you are the Teacher, you are the Owner, you are the one in charge. Your clients addressing you with your title instead of just your first name solidifies that you are higher up in the food chain.

Is the function of your honorific for protocol or for branding?

An honorific like "Daddy" may not invite a client who prefers a more seductive, worshipful type of session, while "Princess" may not fit the vibe you're looking for either. Figure out what purpose your honorific serves whether this is something you will embody or it's a fun marketing quirk.

E.g. Lady Vi commonly goes by The Satanatrix. This honorific has more of a function of branding than it does for use of actual protocol. 'Lady' is the actual honorific used in a session.

The benefits and drawbacks to a unique honorific.

If the standard Mistress, Mistrix, Daddy, Domina, etc. isn't appealing, you may have considered creating an entirely new or rarely used honorific. At its best, this is something that encapsulates your brand without pigeonholing you, or sets you apart as Goddess Jessica vs. Domina Jessica. At its worst, it is something clients have a hard time grasping, using, or understanding.

PRO TIP

Got a client who's used to calling everyone "Mistress" and can't quite nail yours when the blood rushes to their downstairs? Use your name and honorific a lot in session with them, or better yet, have them repeat it. "Bend down and rub Lady Michelle's feet," or "After every spank, you will say 'thank you Domina Diana.'" After a while, it'll be stuck in their heads.

Careful when choosing an honorific that is specific to a niche or activity, as it can limit mobility within the industry. The honorific of "Doctor" might imply you only do med-fet, even though your real passion is wrestling. Changing an honorific mid-career is much easier than changing a name. Though changing a name can and has been done, it can be trickier to navigate.

Don't feel pressure to have an honorific or to adopt higher protocol. Do note that if your potential client prefers or is used to protocol, they may first address you with their honorific of choice. Not having a specified honorific can allow you to be flexible to your client's preferred honorific, as long as it is one that does not offend or insult you personally.

Stuck on which honorific to use?
Circle all that intrigue you from this non-exhaustive list.

MONARCHY

Your Highness

Queen/King

Duchess/Duke

Lady/Lord

Empress/Emperor

Shogun

Sultan

Princess/Prince

CLASSIC

Mommy

Daddy

Mistress/Mistrix

Madam

Domina

Sir

JOBS

Doctor

Coach

Chef

Sergeant

Captain

Madame/Mr President

Boss

Colonel

Admiral

RELIGIOUS

Reverend

Father

Sister

Saint

Rabbi

Your Holiness

Shamanatrix

Goddess

PROOF OF CONCEPT

The whole branding and naming task can feel overwhelming, especially when you factor in that it may change once you start seeing clients or interacting in the space. For that reason, do not feel that you need to perfectly curate your brand before you soft launch it to the world. You do not need a website to start seeing clients or for people to take you seriously. Do not worry about these avenues until you have proof of concept, meaning tangible evidence that this is a path you should invest in— i.e. a client paid you for a session and you didn't hate it. All you truly need to start out is an ad, a booking form, an email address (ideally two), and a social media account (for social proof).

FACE IN VS FACE OUT

"Should I show my face in my ads or on my website?"

This is a question we get asked a LOT, and it's really important to think about for yourself. What's the real cost of showing your face in ads?

Historically, most sex workers have shied away from showing their faces in ads. Even now, take a look at your local ad directory and you'll see cleverly cropped photos, lacy *Eyes Wide Shut* masks, and blur-face filters over half of providers' photos. Why would folks choose to censor their face?

There are a lot of things that can be affected, should someone with nefarious intent get a hold of an ad or a profile that you advertise on, and connect that profile to your civilian life. It's not just the danger of arrest for solicitation. Got kids? A family court judge might think a sex worker is unfit to parent. Colleges often have deeply subjective "morality clauses" buried deep in the student handbook. Pending immigration case? Biometrics and facial recognition are tools wielded by state departments all over the world. Sex workers are widely (and legally!) discriminated against in all kinds of ways. Think about what you have to lose before you decide to post that super hot photo of you wearing a strap-on harness.

It's not just faces, either. Some sex workers go to much further lengths to hide their identity, like wearing wigs and covering up tattoos. There's also the matter of government IDs being required for almost all mainstream ad sites. Some of them report to local governments, leading to issues with immigration, banking, and travel.

Folks with security clearances might want to shy away from posting at all on those ad sites, let alone with their face showing. Concealing your identity isn't being ashamed of who you are— it's a step to achieving your goals, whatever they may be.

FEAR INVENTORY

If I were to get doxxed (legal/government name outed) what does this mean for me and how will I handle this?

FEAR	Why am I afraid?	What is the likelihood of this happening?	What would happen if this fear came true?	Plan of action/ inaction.

HOMEWORK

Look at providers in your area. Pick out three clever or stylized images or poses that conceal the provider's face or body.

HOMEWORK

Come up with a few face-in images or poses that fit with the image your persona projects.

CHAPTER 7: FACE IN FACE OUT

Whether you plan to stay face in forever or are unsure, understanding what you stand to lose can help you make the decision.

> **DO MY ADS SHOW ANY IDENTIFYING INFORMATION ABOUT ME THAT OTHERS MAY RECOGNIZE?**

> **HOW COULD I CONCEAL MY IDENTITY IF I CHOSE TO DO SO?**

> **IF I CHOOSE TO GO FACE OUT, HOW WOULD THIS AFFECT MY CURRENT LIVELIHOOD, FAMILY, OR COMMUNITY?**

ADVERTISING

While it's true that there are enough perverts to spend money on everyone, you also want the *right* perverts to spend money on you. Maybe you're passionate about bondage, but all you get in your inbox are crossdressers. Marketing and branding will help you define your ideal client and for those ideal clients to find you.

Speak the right language

The single most important thing about marketing and branding is that you speak the right language to the right person. Take your brand identity from an earlier exercise, the thing that you *do*. Say you're moody, brooding, and service oriented– you want to write copy that describes that.

Writing copy that feels authentic to your own voice is often daunting. In that regard, practice makes perfect. Try typing out what a session with you is like using sensory words. What are the sights, sounds, and smells of your session? Describe the feelings, both emotional and physical.

PRO TIP

Try googling words in your city that relate to your brand or niche. If you work in New York you can try "Dominatrix NYC," or "Foot Fetish Brooklyn," etc...

CREATING AN AD

Ads are tricky to write, between ad sites getting shuttered (thanks, SESTA/FOSTA) and the heavy restrictions placed on the ones we do have left. Your first attempt at writing an ad will probably get pinged back for "not meeting publishing standards," aka the software that scans for vulgarities thinks you're being too sexy in your advertisement for sexy services on a sexy service platform. It's a tricky line to walk.

DON'T list every kink or activity that you offer. Folks sometimes think "if I don't list everything, the client might not know I offer it!" Since the dawn of time, clients have been asking for services we don't offer, and they will continue to do so until the heat death of the universe. If you list "impact play, OTK, bastinado," that doesn't mean that someone looking for a judicial caning will skip you over as an option.

DO pick six or seven things that get you out of bed in the morning. Talk about the kinks and activities that you love doing and/or are good at, and talk about *why*. Do you love them? Do you love the face of trepidation as someone is held tightly in bondage, the knowledge that you will be using them in whatever way pleases you, or that they are motionless, unable to escape your whims and desires?

DON'T use vague sentences to describe your Dominance. "You will be helpless at my feet" and "I will totally dominate your mind and body" are silly things to say. WHY are they so helpless? HOW will you dominate their mind, body, and bank accounts? Everyone is different, and someone who really gets you as a person is a client you'll be happy to have back time and time again.

DO describe the sensory experience of a session with you. What is the sound of your heels clicking across the wood floor? Is there cold air on the client's butt when you lay them over your lap, warmed up quickly by your strong hand during an OTK (over the knee) spanking? What feelings does your presence inspire? Awe? Gratitude? Fear?

DON'T set them up for failure before they even have a chance to contact you. Have clear protocol for how to contact you, with all of your expectations laid out. Sometimes we see things like "you MUST send tribute BEFORE filling out My application or it WILL go in the trash." While you could, in theory, ask for a large initial fee before you've even taken them on as a client, it will do a heavy amount of filtering out which clients can even get to your email inbox, not to mention it can look like scammy behavior when you're new.

DO describe what your needs are surrounding screening, location, and deposit methods. Mentioning that you do sessions in X location as well as Y location may be enough for someone who lives within driving distance of one of those to book with you.

Fish for touring: You can gauge interest in potential clients located in places you want to tour by mentioning in your ads that you sometimes tour far-flung destinations.

When choosing photos: Anyone can look hot in the lens of a camera (and with Photoshop). What kind of story are you trying to tell? What message do you want to convey? Angles are your friend here. Does the camera point up from your shoes, a glimpse from a submissive on the floor? Will your clients be witnessing your grace from between the bars of a cage?

PRO TIP

Candids and selfies aren't the mark of an amateur. Posting a selfie or a BTS photo tricks the viewer into thinking you're "more authentic" because some clients think we don't have photoshop on our iPhones.

Do you offer sub or switch sessions, where the client may have YOU in the cage? Do you choose to shoot with a submissive or with a prop? Are you doing a conceptual shoot or weird location? And we can't stress this enough…HAVE AT LEAST ONE SELFIE.

WHEN YOU SPEAK TO EVERYONE, YOU SPEAK TO NO ONE

It may feel tempting to cast a wide net to appeal to as many clients as possible, which is fine if you have the time and energy to do performative sessions. While this may appeal to the Dom/me/mx collector, someone who likes your specific look, or plain old NGM, it may feel draining and/or unsatisfying.

> **DESCRIBE YOUR IDEAL CLIENT WITHOUT USING WORDS RELATED TO MONEY.**

IN SUMMARY

1. Keep an eye on your ever changing local laws.
2. Protect what's important to you when making decisions about your advertising.
3. Don't just list activities, tell a story.

CHAPTER 7: MARKETING YOURSELF

Sometimes it's hard to say nice things about yourself, use this worksheet to figure out how to market YOU.

WHAT PLATFORMS DO I PLAN ON USING FOR MARKETING?

WILL I MARKET DIFFERENTLY DEPENDING THE PLATFORM?

WITHOUT USING WORDS LIKE "DOMINATE," "SUBMISSION," OR SPECIFIC ACTIVITIES, HOW WOULD I DESCRIBE A SESSION WITH ME IN A FEW SENTENCES?

WHAT DIFFERENTIATES ME FROM OTHER DOM/ME/MX'S? LIST PHYSICAL AND NON-PHYSICAL ATTRIBUTES.

WHAT IS MY ADVERTISING BUDGET?
(BOTH TIME AND MONEY)

AD SITES I PLAN TO USE

WHAT STORY DO I WANT TO TELL MY CLIENTS THROUGH MY BRANDING? HOW DO I WANT THEM TO FEEL?

HOW WILL I TRACK THE PERFORMANCE ACROSS DIFFERENT AD SITES?

WILL I CHANGE MY AD STRATEGY AND SPEND WHEN TOURING?

HOMEWORK

Describe a spanking in the voice of your brand identity. Use sensory words to describe the before and after.

CHAPTER 8
PRE-SESSION ADMIN

Congrats! You're ready to start taking bookings. This is where the money happens, but will also be the bane of your existence. People will contact you EVERYWHERE. Social media comments, DMs, emails, phone calls, text messages, and calls from your fansites, all demanding one thing: access to you. It's often tempting to answer every inquiry; we all hope that the person behind this new DM is going to be a whale, but it turns out you have to kiss a lot of frogs before the prince shows up.

It's important to figure out what to respond to and how you will set up that process in advance. One of the first interactions you will have with a client is that initial inquiry. Setting clear instructions for them to follow is very important. If they can't follow your rules for communication, how can you expect them to follow your rules in the session?

EMAIL

When you start receiving emails, most of them will be junk. How do you filter out the timewasters from the actual bookings?

Step 1: create an email address. This is going to be public facing, but you will rarely check it.

Step 2: create another email address. This is the one you will use to interface with your clients.

Step 3: Post the first email on your ads.

Step 4: Turn on auto responder (mentioned below) to that first email address.

Step 5: Only check the second email address.

The first email is going to shield you from bots, people who have no intention of booking, and people who are typing with one hand at 4am. We'll let you guess what is in the other hand. Only those who fill out your intake form from your autoresponder will get access to your second email address.

AUTORESPONDERS

Some email platforms allow you to turn on an autoresponder, which is an automatic response to every email sent. You can still send a response to an email later, but the autoresponder delivers information fast. This feature is widely used by many folks, especially on an email address associated with ads.

Thanks for your email, I'd love to talk to you in intimate detail about this, but before we do, please fill out (link to intake form), review my session policies on (link to sessions page on website), and don't forget your (screening information).

XOXO, Domina

You can change up the script as needed.

PRO TIP

Put all your links into the auto responder. Clip or fansites, wishlists, phone/text site, etc. in addition to your own personal website and booking form. If you're not online when their emails come in, they can still see your content or send you a little tip via other platforms.

Many like to build an intake form, which allows the client to fill in all of your requested information. You can ask for whatever you want in this form: the desired length of session, desired activities or fantasies, hard limits, where they found your ad, etc. You can choose what information is mandatory and what is optional, and make it so they won't be able to submit the form until they've provided you with all the info you've asked for. And if they respond N/A to all to all your mandatory requirements, that also tells you about the effort they are willing to make when it comes to your clearly stated needs.

COMMON FORM QUESTIONS

★ Name
★ Email
★ Phone
★ Session type
★ Limits
★ Length of booking
★ References
★ Allergies
★ Age
★ Experience
★ How did you find me
★ Desired city

WHAT BDBC ALUMNI ARE SAYING...

> *A field in my contact form says 'anything else you'd like to mention? I take kindly to compliments'*
> *This tells me what the client was thinking when they filled it out, and why they want to book me.*

GODDESS FLORA SPARKS

Some providers may include gender identity, ethnicity, age, weight, etc. on their intake forms. Shayla used to ask for someone's favorite karaoke jam. You can ask whatever you want, for any reason you want. We want to filter the responses that come in, so you're left only with folks you are *enthusiastic* about seeing.

Now that you have an intake form, it's time to automate.

DIRECTING COMMUNICATION TO THE APPROPRIATE CHANNELS

Being hot on the internet generally means your inbox can be a dumpster fire of time wasters, bots, and offers for sex toy reviews. Most of these aren't worth the effort to answer, but spending a little time panning the river can come up with gold. This doesn't mean giving attention to every "hey" message. You want to direct potential clients as quickly as possible to the right platforms, where you can be open about kinks and fantasies, and open about getting paid for it. It is *never* a good idea to negotiate IRL sessions or talk in depth about fantasies in social media DMs or on fan sites. These communications often run afoul of each individual site's terms of service and can get you banned. Instead, try answering the DMs with some of these responses:

"I'd love to talk to you in-depth about this, why don't you shoot me an email at yourname@yourdomain.com"

"For more information about me, you can check out my website www.website.com, there's lots of photos and links there"

"That sounds awesome— let's migrate this over to (link to fansite) so I can show you what I'm thinking."

Copy and paste these liberally.

WHAT WILL MY CANNED RESPONSES SAY?

VETTING

Many sex workers screen their clients. You might see "light screening" listed on advertisements. You may see "references required" on a contact form. What does this mean?

Screening is how sex workers keep themselves safe. Screening is done in many different ways, each with their own pros and cons. Every provider will take a different approach to screening. Some will be more relaxed or have minimal screening, while others are more extensive. This is entirely dependent on your risk profile.

As a note: screening methods and sites vary widely based on locale and specifics are not listed here. To find screening in your own area, reach out to providers in your area and ask what they're using.

References: This means the client has seen a provider before, and lists their contact information for you to verify. You'll contact the provider, and they'll verify that they've seen the client, and whether or not the client behaved themselves. Some will offer more information that you might need to know, some might be a little more discreet. The benefit of this is that you get information from a real human about whether or not the client is safe. The downside is sometimes clients are Dr. Jekyll with one provider, and Mr. Hyde with another.

Work Screening: Some providers require a photo ID that matches up with a social media profile or a public-facing employee listing. Some go as far as to call their place of employment and ask to speak to the client by name. This does verify that the client is a real person and you have their legal name, but doesn't tell you anything about the safety or reliability of the client.

Blacklists: Your local area probably has what's called a "bad date list" or a community blacklist that contains notes on bad/unsafe clients. You can plug in the information of your potential client and see if they show up. This can help keep you from seeing a bad client, but no news isn't always good news– blacklists aren't comprehensive and all-knowing.

Keep in mind, while screening can save lives, it's not bulletproof.

NEVER SHARE BLACKLIST OR REFERENCE INFO WITH A CLIENT. If there's bad entries on there, but the client has been nothing but peaches and cream with you, do **not** pass along that information to any client. This puts all of our safety at tremendous risk.

THE EMAILS ARE ENDLESS. HERE'S HOW TO STOP THEM.

Once you've got the information from their contact form and finished screening, it's time to nail down the time, place, and rate. This is where getting a deposit comes in. Hairdressers, caterers, mechanics, etc. all charge deposits; why would we be any different?

Providers have different strategies for deposits. Some take a % of the total booking, some take a flat fee. Only you know what's right for you. The methods of deposit can be anything you want. Money transfer apps like Venmo or CashApp are common, but be careful of what goes in the subject line lest your account gets shut down for "fraudulent activity." Some clients don't like to leave a paper trail and prefer to buy a physical gift card with cash at a local drugstore. If this is the case, always verify the card works before agreeing to see the client.

Be careful to choose methods where your government name isn't front and center whenever possible. The methods of screening, deposits, references you choose are entirely up to your risk profile. There is no foolproof method, only the system that feels good and works for *you*.

Cancellations: A wise full service worker once said "It's a miracle how car crashes happen way less and fewer grandmothers die the very day of our meeting once the deposit amount increases." The joke here is that clients sometimes treat our meetings as disposable and make up a lie to cancel. If you've got a deposit in hand, it's a lot harder for them to flake, as they now have skin in the game. If there's a legitimate reason to cancel, some providers will allow the client to move their deposit to another day and time, but others keep that deposit as a cancellation fee. Only you can decide what's right for you and your business. If you are the one canceling, offer to reschedule to another day, or ask the client how they'd like their deposit back.

Sometimes, they throw a wrench in your map of Contact Form > Screen > Deposit > Session by sending a bunch of verbose, fantasy-filled emails along the way. It's your job to keep them in line. Guide them gently towards better behavior by setting boundaries and offering options.

COMMON PAIN POINTS

They send multiple emails asking what you're gonna do to them

"It sounds like your fantasy is very detailed. Let's talk about it on (phone or cam site)"

They can't figure out a time

Some providers have calendar links or ask for 3 times and days that work for the client.

They won't send a deposit

They love the illusion of control. Give them options like a toddler. "You can choose to send the deposit via method one or method two"

They won't screen

Trust your gut here. Screening methods are different for everyone, and the client might be open to a different way of screening or they might not. It's 100% okay (and encouraged!) to say "at this time I cannot accommodate new friends who can't fulfill my screening requirements."

They send endless emails without booking

When they inevitably respond to that DM or email message with some time waster behavior like "oh but I just wanted to blah blah blah," you can copy paste the exact same response you gave earlier. Some of them think they're talking to a bot at that point and it's funny. You can also consider pretending you are your own assistant to interact with your clientele via email. If they can't follow your instructions, they don't get to book. Full stop. They keep sending emails? You don't have to read them. They bother you on other platforms? You can ignore/block.

PRO TIP

Become your own assistant! Introduce yourself off the bat with "Hi! I'm (assistant name) and I'll be assisting you with the booking process for (Dom/me/mx name). To get started, they require everybody fill out this form, send this deposit, etc. Sometimes people get a whole lot nicer when they think there is a "bouncer" between them and you.

HONING IN ON YOUR IDEAL CLIENT

We all will have a different filtration process. The more rigorous and specific our process is, the more we filter out. That can be a good thing if you are looking for something very *specific*. It also means less people to sift through. While an emptier email inbox is music to everyone's ears, it also means less volume. So if you are more niche, there may be longer periods of waiting between client inquiries, but those clients will be a better match for your specific interests.

PRO TIP

If you truly can't afford to turn down a client and as a result engage in a looser screening process, always try to meet in a more public space like a coffee shop, or session in a rental dungeon or in-call where someone else is on the premises. There is safety in numbers and you can get a better read on the client in person before going alone into a room with them.

Your standards and system for screening and booking can be as tight or as loose as you want. No one can take this away from you. But know that the more you filter, the more clientele you self-select out. This, ultimately, is a cool thing, as our ideal stable of clients are folks who would jump through ANY hoop for us. Unfortunately, those clients take time to find when you're new. Make your funnel wider if you need more volume. Over time, you can increase your filters.

Know that you may ask for all of these things before the booking process is complete and they may not comply with any of it. These are the risks you run before you see the client, which is why we stress not wasting unnecessary energy on clients pre-deposit or pre-session.

IN SUMMARY

1. Your admin work should work for you, not the other way around.
2. We build these systems to make our lives easier, not harder.
3. Screening doesn't have to be scary.

CHAPTER 8: PRE SESSION ADMIN

Pre-session admin will be the most annoying thing you have to do, but it is also the most important. Plan out the flow using these questions.

WHAT TASKS CAN I AUTOMATE?

WHERE AM I NOTICING A DROP OFF WITH CONVERTING CLIENTS?

WHAT DAYS OF THE WEEK WILL I DEDICATE TO DOING ALL THE UN-SEXY ADMIN WORK?

ADMIN TASKS I LIKE DOING	ADMIN TASKS I HATE DOING

HOW WILL I MAKE ADMIN WORK SUCK LESS? CO-WORK WITH COLLEAGUES? KILLER PLAYLISTS? REWARD MYSELF WITH A TREAT?

CHAPTER 8: EMAIL, VETTING, SCREENING

Emails, vetting, and screening may feel like the bane of your existence but they are necessary for you survival.

WHAT ARE MY MOST IMPORTANT BOOKING FORM QUESTIONS?

WHAT SCREENING METHODS ARE AVAILABLE TO ME?

HOW WILL I KNOW WHEN IT'S TIME TO TAKE A BREAK?

HOMEWORK

Create two email addresses: one you will use for emailing, and the other is for advertising and/or autoresponder.

HOMEWORK

Create a booking form! You can use airtable, jot forms, or something comparable.

HOMEWORK

Write a template for reference requests. Don't forget a template for thanking the giver after they respond!

CHAPTER 9

ASKING FOR WHAT YOU WANT

CHAPTER 9
RELEVANT 7DOD CLASSES

Sensual FinDom with Faustine Cox (Volume IV)

High Protocol with Sinclair Sexsmith (Volume X)

No. (The Art of Denial) with Ashley Paige (Volume V)

You have the vision of the Dom/me/mx: long legs, sexy, corseted, whip wielding. "DROP TO THE FLOOR" they yell at a cowering submissive, who drops to his knees immediately. This is a pretty visceral image, right? Make demands, get what you want. But it doesn't always play out that way.

Having too many demands is a trap many newbies fall into. Demands have their place, certainly, but making demands right off the bat is often a turnoff for many folks. Something, something, *catch more flies with honey* and all that. But there's no need to be sweet when asking for something you want. You can harness power using both direct and indirect asks.

DIRECT VS INDIRECT ASKS

Direct asks are exactly what they sound like: "I would like you to buy this for me" or "drop to your knees and hold out your palms in front of you." These are simple instructions asked directly to someone else. The other person can either comply with the ask, or go in a different direction.

Indirect asks are things we expect of someone *before* they get something else. Clients are asked to fill out a booking form *before* they're allowed to communicate directly about a session. A sign at a shoe store indicating where the line starts in front of the cash register is an IRL example of an indirect ask. The store is asking you to stand in a specific place and wait until they're ready to ring you up, all without having to utter a single word.

We often don't ask for what we want because of fear. Fear that we will lose something important. We fear hurting someone's feelings, and fear that they will never return to session with us. We fear looking "less dominant" because we've asked for something that we want or need. We fear even asking the questions because the answer to them might be a resounding no.

Utilizing the power of indirect asks in session means not only do we get what we want, but we also get clients who are enthusiastic about giving it to us, in a way that doesn't spark that fear of losing our power or established dynamic.

> *If you ask in a way that is dominant, get spacious and non-judgmental. Say they can't fulfill a request, they're not going to feel bad about it, because you're not going to judge them, you're just going to say "That is all right. I will ask another pet."*

**FROM SENSUAL FINDOM
WITH FAUSTINE COX (VOLUME IV)**

Perhaps you want your client to worship your boots in a certain way, or always bring you an iced coffee before sessions. Lay this out in your protocol, your marketing, or your session itself. Sensually direct your client to gently kiss rather than slobber on your toes in the moment, or tell them that the best way to get you into topspace is by thinking about how they can't help their desire for you while waiting in the Dunkin' drive thru.

What happens when a client says no? Maybe they forget your coffee in a rush to get to your session, or they get so worked up by the sight of your toes that they forget all protocol. You have two options: teach them protocol or give them punishment.

Protocol means instructions and training– you instruct them in the way they should go, and then they follow the instructions. Perhaps this means they repeat the activity or action over and over until they get it right. Eroticize this, make it known that if they do exactly what you want, they will get more of what they like.

Punishment: if this is a new relationship, a sudden spanking for not following instructions may be confusing if not previously negotiated, and sometimes folks act up to get more punishment or funishment (see: brats). It's also very important to identify what sort of punishment works best. A spanking might not be much punishment for a masochist; being sent out in lacy panties under jeans to get your coffee might be a much more effective one.

ON PROTOCOL

Protocol can be an effective tool to highlight power dynamics within a relationship without asking, but it's something that needs to be built intentionally.

> *Tasks and rituals can bring more consciousness and intention to the dynamic. Protocols can make it feel like there is more power and things to do with that power. Protocols can set up my submissive for success and I want them to succeed rather than to set them up to fail or as an excuse for punishment.*

**FROM HIGH PROTOCOL
WITH SINCLAIR SEXSMITH (VOLUME XI)**

Have you ever said "get on your knees" and been greeted by a myriad of interpretations? It's not always sexy or efficient to correct someone after the fact. We often leave our commands or instructions too vague. "Worship my feet" can mean anything from drooling on toes, to words of adoration from a disciple who dares not touch. Our jobs are not only to deliver clear instructions from the get-go, but to instill confidence in our clients that they're pleasing us by doing a good job.

PRO TIP

There's heaps of literature on position training, much of which is based on scenes from a series of sci-fi books released in the 60's. Search "Gorean Slave Positions" to find a handy dandy chart of poses to teach your submissive for easy access to their bodies and even easier access to their minds.

Using protocol with specific instructions, you get what you want and need the first time. "Get down on both knees with your head bowed and your palms facing up" is a clear order, with no room for interpretation. You get the position you want, and your client knows that they've followed your instructions perfectly. This takes practice. In the beginning you may not intuitively know how to get clients to do what you want seamlessly. Keeping at it is best, and don't forget the big picture.

All of your needs may not be met by one client, but what needs are they meeting? Where do they fit within the *Whore Hierarchy of Needs*?

CREATIVELY, FINANCIALLY
EMOTIONALLY SATISFIED.

DOES THIS CLIENT HELP ME GROW?
DO I FEEL INSPIRED
OR EXCITED TO SEE THIS CLIENT?

DO I FEEL VALUED?
DO I FEEL GOOD
AFTER OUR SESSIONS?

DOES THIS CLIENT
DRAIN ME EMOTIONALLY?

ARE WE GETTING PAID
FOR THE SERVICES
RENDERED AND
NOBODY GOT HURT?

WHORE HIERARCHY OF NEEDS

IN SUMMARY

1. Don't stop asking for things because you are afraid of hearing the word no.
2. Punishment and funishment are two separate beasts.
3. You can get everything you want, you just have to ask.

CHAPTER 9: ASKING FOR WHAT YOU WANT

Getting exactly what you want is a muscle that needs to be flexed. Think about what you want as you move through these questions

DESCRIBE A TIME WHEN YOU ASKED FOR, AND RECEIVED, SOMETHING YOU WANTED:

WAS IT VIA DIRECT OR INDIRECT ASK?

HOW DID IT MAKE THE GIVER FEEL?

WHAT ARE YOU CURRENTLY IMPLEMENTING IN YOUR PRACTICE?

DIRECT ASKS

INDIRECT ASKS

WHAT BEHAVIORS OR PROTOCOLS DO I WANT FROM MY CLIENTS?

HOW WILL I ASK FOR THIS DIRECTLY OR INDIRECTLY?

WHAT WILL I DO IF THEY DO NOT COMPLY?

HOMEWORK

Write a few sample asks in a direct and an indirect format.

I.E. you want the client to remove their shoes upon entering.

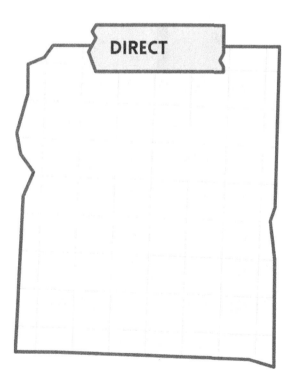

DIRECT

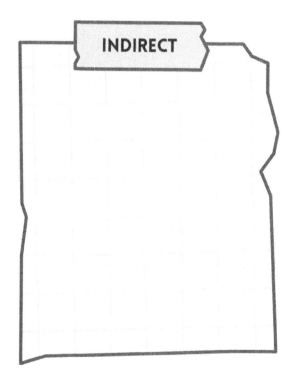

INDIRECT

CHAPTER 10
NEGOTIATION

> **CHAPTER 10**
> **RELEVANT 7DOD CLASSES**
>
> *Exercising Inclusivity in Consent Negotiation*
> *with Vivienne Vai (Volume II)*
>
> *Going Beyond Yes, No, Maybe*
> *with Princess Kali (Volume VI)*
>
> *Embodied Boundaries*
> *with Vivienne Vai (Volume VIII)*

> *Negotiations give us a space to give and receive the necessary information that we need to play safely with each other. It is also an opportunity for us to connect before we play, to build rapport to get a sense of the other person's energy before playing.*

FROM INCLUSIVITY IN NEGOTIATION
WITH VIVIENNE VAI (VOLUME II)

The first thing to understand in a kink negotiation is that this process is more synonymous with a conversation or clarification of boundaries and actions, rather than a zero-sum game. Negotiation does not mean one party compromises with the other, but instead ensures sure both you and your client are on the same page, and that both parties can be assured each of you can act autonomously during the session.

> *It is an idealistic idea that any communication diminishes excitement. Frankly, submissives are big perpetrators of this idea. Kink is a team sport. Negotiation is an ongoing experience. Consent is an ongoing experience.*

**FROM GOING BEYOND YES, NO, MAYBE
WITH PRINCESS KALI (VOLUME VI)**

Negotiation is an opportunity to determine what type of language and processes the two of you will use. This is a great time for clarification, as we all may have different definitions of the same word, or can exhibit emotions differently. What looks like respect to one Dominant may be completely different to another. What looks like enjoyment by one client may be indifference in another. Sometimes this can solely be determined by you; other times it may be more of a collaboration. In any case, you want to provide plenty of opportunities for autonomy for your client. Since you are responsible for setting your own boundaries and ground rules as a professional, this can easily slip into a space where the client is only following your rules and potentially compromising their own autonomy, boundaries, and desires.

This doesn't mean you are to acquiesce to your client's every need, but you do need to hear them out or give them room to express without retaliation. To avoid fielding openly misogynistic, racist, or any other type of harmful or annoying requests all day, we encourage you to develop your own questionnaire, intake form, or discussion process to both filter out the time wasters and boundary pushers, and also to help give them the words more than 'completely dominate me,' 'sensual fun,' and 'whatever pleases Mistress.' This can look like fill-in-the-blanks, empty checkboxes, or a verbal discussion. The format is up to you.

> *Negotiations are a cross between cruising, ordering from the longest dessert menu you've ever seen in your life, running through a pilot's pre-flight checklist, and seeing a new therapist for the first time where you have to summarize all of your childhood trauma for somebody you've never met.*

**FROM INCLUSIVITY IN NEGOTIATION
WITH VIVIENNE VAI (VOLUME II)**

FEELINGS VS ACTIVITIES

We've gotten the questionnaire responses that solely lead with the genitals more times than we can count, so we've developed a **KINK FEELINGS CHART** for your client to choose the feeling(s) they would like to experience during and/or after play. You can find this in the back of the workbook.

While a list of activities you're going to do with the client can certainly be useful, desired feelings can both inform the activities you are to engage in as well as suggest other activities that may not have been on their shortlist. An adoring pegging is going to be much different than a degrading one! And if an adoring pegging is not on the list of experiences you provide, perhaps you can suggest some adoring domestic servitude or adoring pet play. For more ideas on how feelings and activities can pair up see **CHAPTER 11: First Time Sessions for Idiots.**

WHEN DO YOU NEGOTIATE?

Negotiation can and should happen in more than just a single conversation. You can start as early as your intake form (see **CHAPTER 8**). This also provides you with an opportunity to get them thinking about how they want to feel well before the session as well as the proper language– your language– to communicate with each other. Give them the tools they need to be the best client for you. Every Dom/me/mx is different, so provide readily available information about your expectations early and often.

BEFORE THE SESSION

Pre-session is a good time to get clear on their wishlist of activities/scenarios. Use this to cross reference both what you are willing to do, as well as what you are willing to do to them. You don't have to tick all your client's boxes in one session— or at all. You can have your own boundaries of when you will do certain scenes and activities in your relationship with each client (i.e., no butt stuff in first sessions). Do you have a ritual that you do with all first-time clients and it doesn't matter what they want? Great. The more non-negotiables you have, the more you should make them aware within the preliminary stages. This wastes less time for *both* of you.

In addition to your intake form, you can use that pre-session time for them to marinate on questions and supply you with the answers come session time. For example: How will I know when you're enjoying something? What are your bodily responses/behaviors to __? What does aftercare look like for you? What are words or actions that would make you turn off? Do you have any no-go words?

DURING THE SESSION

Even if you've negotiated beforehand, it's a good idea to get a gut check before each session, even if you've played with them before. You can do this simply with a verbal check-in, or go a step further by walking them through everything that will happen as well as how they can communicate with you during. This is a great tool for first time clients, or those entirely new to sessioning with you or in general. That doesn't mean you have to walk them through *every* painstaking detail, phrase, or activity; just give a general overview.

Example: "I'm going to ask you a variety of questions to start out. I'm not looking for any particular answer from you, so try not to tell me what you think I want to hear. I always want your honest answer. Then I'm going to ask you to strip naked. When you do this, you are not to touch me. I'm going to use a few tools to cause an impact on your body. If anything hurts too much, you can say yellow or stomp your foot. I will only gradually increase my intensity, so you don't have to worry about me going from 0 to 60 at warp speed."

AFTERCARE

If you come from a lifestyle kink background, you may be utterly surprised at how many clients are interested in minimal aftercare.

Yep, they just had things inserted in their pee hole and were bleeding from their thighs, yet they just waltz right back into their corporate job by squeezing this 90 minutes of terror and sadism into their goddamn lunch break.

The point is: YOU can require a certain level of aftercare for your client, especially if you had a scene involving edge play or that was particularly heavy. Aftercare as a professional looks much different than it does in kinky lifestyle settings.

Just like in your negotiations, aftercare should not be done "in character." You can code-switch at this time to simply provider instead of Dominatrix.

Aftercare in a professional setting can look like:

- ★ Being human: chatting, having a nice, out-of-scene conversation as equals. This could be about anything, from the session to the weather.
- ★ Physical needs: getting them a glass of water or tending to any wounds.
- ★ Acknowledgement or thanks: "thank you for sharing your body with me during this hour/5 hour/entire week etc."

Do I include aftercare after the session or bake that into their session time?

That's up to you. Most of us bake it in because that is still part of the service you are providing (and encourages them to make longer bookings). Though, perhaps it's also why they waltz out in their 3 piece suit sans aftercare to their board meetings.

You probably need aftercare too. Top Drop can be intense, even for professionals. Aftercare can be anything that restores you to sanity.

Consider:

- ★ A playlist that makes you feel good and/or relax meditation or a quick yoga flow.
- ★ "Thank you" emails (see **CHAPTER 17**)
- ★ Closing rituals, such as cleaning or a certain snack post session.

IN SUMMARY

Negotiations with clients aren't a high-stakes game of back and forth. It can and *should* be an ongoing process to discuss wants and needs through direct or indirect communication. This is how you get to know your client and their expectations of you–and vice versa–so you may come together to build scenes beyond your wildest dreams.

CHAPTER 10: NEGOTIATION

Negotiation occurs at many different touchpoints, use this worksheet to understand what information you'd like from them and when.

WHAT INFORMATION DO I WANT/NEED FROM SOMEONE BEFORE WE SESSION?	**HOW MUCH AND WHAT TYPE OF AFTERCARE AM I WILLING TO PROVIDE?**
WHAT INFO THAT I WANT/NEED CAN ONLY COME FROM WITHIN A SESSION?	**WHAT INFO HELPS ME CRAFT A BETTER SCENE FOR MY CLIENTS?**

HOMEWORK

Create a script for your pre-session negotiation.

CHAPTER 11
FIRST TIME SESSIONS FOR IDIOTS

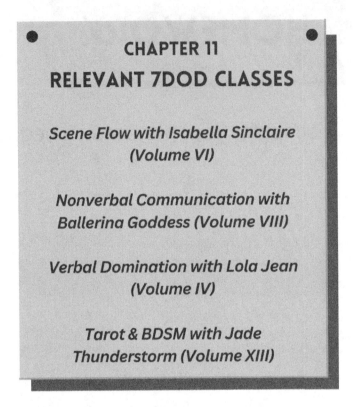

We all have them, and you will too: clients who don't know what they want or how to get there. The client who says their only limits are blood, sounding, or even no limits at all...but you know there is probably more than that. Their idea of telling you what they want is: "Dom/me/mx me, please!" By teaching you how to cut the bullshit and plan a session that benefits both of you, you can tackle any session, physical or mental.

The goal of this first-time session for idiots is to give your client a taste of what they want (domination) while allowing them space to learn what they like, without it being thrust upon them. While your specialties can certainly influence the session, this also gives you more room to learn about the client without worrying about crossing their boundaries, since they probably can't articulate them yet anyways.

Keep in mind that this is entirely optional. You are under no obligation to be a client's first session OR to session with someone who can't articulate their desires/boundaries to your standards.

Three suggestions for this type of intro sessions:

SCENE BUILDING EXERCISE
GREATEST HITS
PROCESS TO MENTAL OR PHYSICAL VULNERABILITY

OPTION 1 - SCENE BUILDING EXERCISE

If you are lucky enough to have a client who can tell you what tools they want to use or how they want to feel during/after the session in more words than "turned on" or "horny," this scene building exercise can work wonders for you! You may find it helpful to give examples before you work on this together, or give this as homework before the session.

Within the **feelings** category, write a feeling they would like to experience (use our *KINK FEELINGS CHART* for suggestions!). In the **tool** category, list the tools, equipment, or items they are curious about. Using this equation, you can decide which activities you can do together to drive your session and inform an **activity**. This is a great exercise to assure both of you are on the same page; as your client attempts to verbalize their desires, you can make sure you have clearly agreed-upon definitions for what each word and activity means.

SCENE BUILDING

FEELING	TOOL	ACTIVITY
Degraded	Strap-on	Slut Training
Used	Paddle	Target Practice
Scared	Rope	Predicament Bondage

OPTION 2 - GREATEST HITS

Maybe your client has given you one thing they want to do, but there's no way you can possibly do just *that* for an hour. Maybe your client has given you absolutely nothing. This is where your greatest hits come in. Think about the activities you feel the most confident doing, the tools you feel most comfortable using, and the words or phrases you feel confident and comfortable throwing at them.

Just because you have the equipment or tool doesn't mean you have to use it. This is a great teaching moment! Describe the tools, show and tell them, and tell your client what you can do with said tool and how it works. If there is ever a lull, this is a great filler.

> *Even if there are pauses you want that pause to be an intentional pause, not a 'what the fuck am I gonna do next' kind of pause. Do you need water? Do you need to rest your legs? Do you need to put your arms down? Do you need to get off your knees? Those are kinds of policies, but it's still a very controlling thing.*

FROM SCENE FLOW WITH ISABELLA SINCLAIRE (VOLUME VI)

Consider what transitions easily. If the only request is something that will involve lube, plan to do your rope activities or anything you don't want to be covered in slime *before* you get the ooey-gooey stuff out. Think of this as assembling a session playlist of things that flow seamlessly into the next...and maybe even create an ACTUAL playlist with audio cues to help you transition to the next activity.

> *Going into a scene is like playing chess. You don't just want to be three steps ahead, but prepared for all the possible variables and situations so that you can maneuver and be flexible. You can only do this if you have a wider understanding of what they need.*

**FROM PRESENCE AND DEMEANOR
WITH NEENA DE VILLE (VOLUME I)**

OPTION 3 - PHYSICAL AND MENTAL VULNERABILITY

Having trouble finding any emotion, activity, or boundary to inform you? Sounds like this person has a lot to learn before you can even feel comfortable guiding them...so let them guide you unknowingly, while they learn. These are processes that lead to vulnerability, which will ultimately help them feel submissive. What you will uncover is: what does submission feel like for them?

The Process to Physical Vulnerability: Sensation Inventory*

We can't assume everyone wants to feel pain. For many newer submissives, pain is something they are scared to encounter. Perhaps this submissive *does* discover a love of pain; this process still leaves room to figure that out. In this example, you are going to do a sensation inventory. Think doctor, medical intake type of vibe. You are going to do a series of tests on their body to see how it responds. Your goal is for them to feel as good as possible. But in order for you to register their responsiveness, they will need to use their body and/or noises to communicate this– no words. The limitation of verbal cues limits the likelihood of topping from the bottom, while providing you with space to influence, encourage, and learn their nonverbal communication. Perhaps you want them to make a specific noise to signify a certain feeling– that's up to you! This will not only teach them to jive with your preferred communication style, but also gets them comfortable communicating with you and having that communication not only respected but *rewarded*. You can use a series of implements, your hands, let your imagination run wild. This also doubles as a learning exercise as you can describe the tools that you're using either before or as you introduce them.

*This is an activity that pairs very well with sensory deprivation and/or nudity as both also encourage physical vulnerability.

The Process to Mental Vulnerability: The Hot Seat Interrogation

Perhaps you're not as comfy with your physical repertoire, or you don't have enough tools for the sensation inventory. Maybe you just like poking around in someone's brain. A hot seat interrogation can be a great jumping off point. It can be helpful to state your intentions at the start of the interrogation.

I.E. "I want to get to know you intimately. That is my goal with this session. Do you want me to know you intimately?"

The idea of this scene is to learn more about them while keeping them off-balance, eventually leading to a mental vulnerability where you are leading/in control. You can choose to add in some sensory deprivation (blindfold, restraints etc...) in order to add to that vulnerability, which you can remind them of– *i.e., "Remember who can see and move freely. I'll give you a hint: it's not you."*

There are different things you may be looking for during a hot-seat interrogation:

★ Bring attention to any physical discomfort.
  ○ I.E. *"I noticed you hesitated, is there a reason this makes you nervous?"*
★ Create a dynamic that throws them off balance by interrupting them.
★ You're looking for interesting information you can expose. This could be about their fantasies, about what they want but may not yet know they want.
★ Start with a few easier, softball questions before getting to the juicy stuff.
★ Layering questions is a technique used by interviewers. The first response tends to be more of a superficial answer. Continue to ask questions on top of that until you get deeper.

What does this look like in action?

You hesitated before you responded, is there a reason why?

Why do you find tall women more dominant?

When did this start?

Do you think that finding women taller than you attractive is a good thing?

Interesting, why do you think that?

What do you find attractive in a Dominant?....and why is that?....why do you think that is?...do you think other people think that too?

You don't have to fill all gaps with questions or conversation. You can simply repeat their answers (as many times as you like). You can use silence to keep them on edge, or you can repeat the same questions over and over, possibly receiving different answers each time.

PRO TIP

Interrogation can be sensual or scary, playful or maniacal. Try softening it with physical touch, blindfolding them so they don't expect your warm caress. Or play a deranged serial killer and give a scary laugh at seemingly innocuous answers. Both scenarios throw them off their game.

It is important to be the one asking and/or controlling the questions in this hot seat interrogation. If they turn a question back to you, possible diversions include:

You seem to be deflecting the questions away from yourself, why do you think you're doing that? Do you usually do this?

It's interesting that you want to know so much about me when it's you who we're learning about.

It seems you're diverting from the question. What do you have to hide?

If you're ever unsure how to respond you can always use silence, or simple phrases like "interesting," "really," or "would you like to answer that again?"

Need a more concrete example? Look up the "football is fun" scene from *Remember the Titans* to see it in action

IN SUMMARY

Don't be frazzled when a client comes to you with nothing. You sometimes have to drag it out of them by supplying them with feeling words, or poking them with your fingers and sticks untill they spill the beans.

CHAPTER 11: FIRST TIME SESSIONS FOR IDIOTS

When they give you no information but you still need to get that bag, figure out what you have in your back pocket.

WILL I/HOW WILL I TAKE SESSIONS WHERE MY CLIENT DOESN'T GIVE ME ENOUGH INFORMATION ABOUT THEIR INTERESTS?

WHAT ACTIVITIES DO I FEEL MOST CONFIDENT IN?

WHICH CAN I INCLUDE MY "SESSION PLAYLIST?"

WHAT TOOLS (EMOTIONAL OR PHYSICAL) ARE IN MY SENSATION INVENTORY BAG?

DO I NEED SPECIAL PREP FOR ANY OF MY FIRST TIME SESSION FOR IDIOT ACTIVITIES?

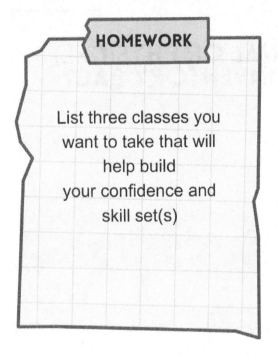

HOMEWORK

List three classes you want to take that will help build your confidence and skill set(s)

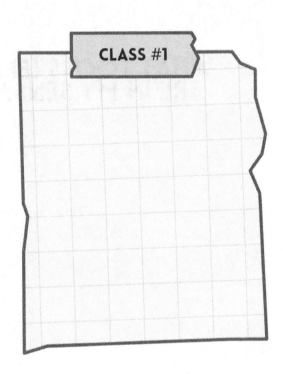

CLASS #1

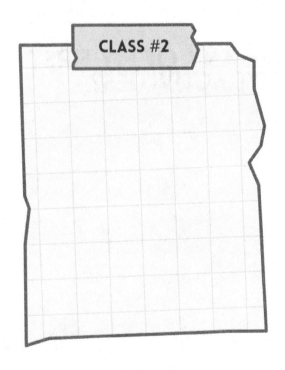

CLASS #2

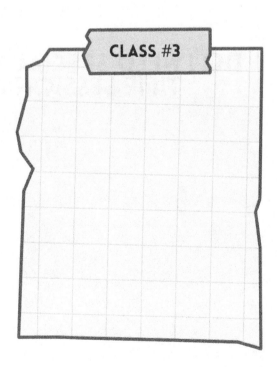

CLASS #3

CHAPTER 12
WHEN SESSIONS GO WRONG

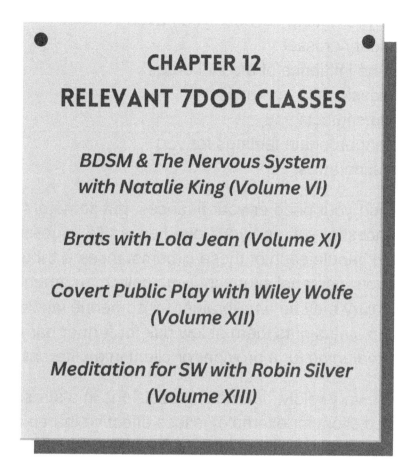

Better to plan to fail than fail to plan, amiright? No matter how much you plan or prepare, not every exchange will go as planned. Your corset pops five minutes in, the dungeon gets raided, client has a heart attack in session, etc. There are so many more things that can go wrong, and you need to be prepared. It's far better to expect the worst and be pleasantly surprised.

A common acronym you should familiarize yourself with in BDSM is RACK: **Risk-Aware Consensual Kink**. Being risk aware goes beyond the hard skills and knowledge to avoid causing harm within a scene. Being truly risk aware means that you know and acknowledge the risks that come with sex work, and in some places it's not pretty.

Possible elements and situations that can go wrong:

- ★ Client no-shows when you've booked a rental space
- ★ Health conditions
- ★ Client seems dangerous or unhinged
- ★ Client thinks they're getting services you haven't offered
- ★ Repeated boundary crosser
- ★ Client is under the influence of alcohol/drugs
- ★ Boring as hell session/the energy is off
- ★ Vengeful ex-wife contacts you
- ★ They develop inappropriate feelings for you
- ★ There is a raid/sting/arrest

Some of these only hurt your pride or your finances, but some of these have huge real-world consequences for you and your loved ones. It's impossible to give instructions for how to handle each of these circumstances without knowing the local laws in your area or your personal situation. E.g.: calling an ambulance to the dungeon to treat an injury may be a no-brainer for someone whose race/class/immigration status puts them at low risk for further harm or arrest, but it can be *literally life threatening* for a provider or client in a different situation.

The reactions to these vary wildly, but making decisions in a stressful situation (in a room with an unhinged client for example) is less effective than making an "exit plan" before the bad thing happens. Think of it like a fire drill– better to know the map to the nearest exit *before* the fire breaks out, rather than identifying the exits while the flames build up around you.

PRO TIP

There are free classes on 7daysofdomination.com that cover first aid for clients and contacting first responders if an emergency happens. Getting Red Cross certified to use an AED will put you and everyone around you at ease.

Identify your biggest fears (or within the horror stories of others) and break it down. What about this event scares you? What does it affect down the line? What systems can you put in place to alleviate some of these fears? Can you get verbal confirmation at the beginning of your session? Would tighter screening help alleviate your fears? How can your network help you? Brainstorm with your colleagues what they would do in this situation. What do you have to lose, and is it worth it?

PRO TIP

If you have an incall or dungeon space: keep popsicles in the freezer for a refreshing way to help out a lightheaded or low blood sugar client.

THE GO BAG

Getting familiar with first aid is an easy thing to do that can take your sessions from "total nightmare" to "slight detour." Keeping inexpensive items like antibacterial wound cream, bandaids, burn cream, antihistamines and glucose tablets in your bag are a quick fix for scrapes, scratches, and sneezing fits. Ice dumped into a ziploc bag serves as a take-home cold pack for busted balls. Carrying narcan and test strips (even if you don't use them!) are literal lifesavers.

IN SUMMARY

It is better to plan to fail than fail to plan. Building a robust and thorough emergency plan before anything bad happens can ease your anxieties and build your confidence.

CHAPTER 12: WHEN SESSIONS GO WRONG

You know what to do when they go right, now it's time to prepare your mental and physical go bag for when they go wrong.

IS THIS TYPE OF WORK LEGAL/DECRIMINALIZED/BANNED AS FUCK IN MY AREA?

WOULD AN ARREST JEOPARDIZE MY FAMILY, DAY JOB, OR OTHER PARTS OF MY LIFE?

HOW WILL I HANDLE "DAMAGE CONTROL" WITH MY CLIENT OR MYSELF?

WHAT MEDICAL INFORMATION DO I NEED FROM MY CLIENT, IF ANY?	**CAN I RELY ON "BACKUP" IN THE FORM OF DUNGEON MANAGEMENT OR NEIGHBORS/FRIENDS NEARBY IN CASE OF EMERGENCY?**
DO I ENGAGE IN ANY TYPE OF EDGE PLAY THAT COULD RESULT IN PHYSICAL OR MENTAL HARM TO MY CLIENT?	**WHAT RITUALS I WILL USE FOR SELF-AFTERCARE AFTER A BAD SESSION?**

FEAR INVENTORY

When shit goes awry, what's your plan of action?

FEAR/PROBLEM	Why am I afraid?	What is the likelihood of this happening?	What would happen if this fear came true?	Plan of action/inaction.
Sting/raid/arrest				
Injury				

HOMEWORK

Create an "OOPS!" kit to put in your session bag.

Include things like Bandaids, Neosporin, or glucose tablets.

CHAPTER 13
PERSONAS, STYLES, NICHES

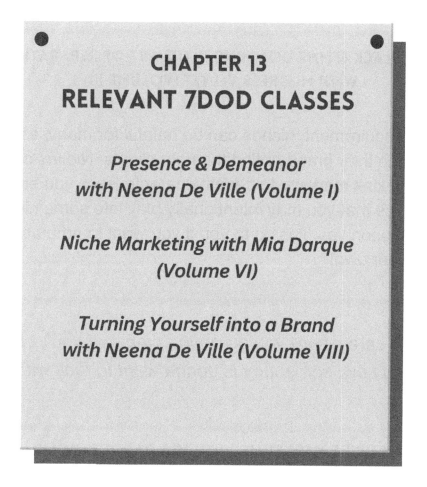

DO YOU NEED A NICHE?

When people first hear about niches, they often think they have to choose one as soon as they start out, or that a niche is critical for success. Neither is true. You don't need to operate in a niche to find success. You don't need to operate in a niche, period. Though, there are circumstances where finding a niche can be helpful.

As you become more experienced, or known for certain traits or activities, the niche will often find you. You don't want to pigeonhole yourself before you discover the thing(s) you're really good at and/or the thing(s) you absolutely love, so there is no need to determine this early on.

> *If you're new to this, build your presence first. When I marketed as a black femme supremacist, someone that was gonna make you read text... I wasn't making a lot of money. I had to rely on, 'I'm your African exotic goddess, come kiss my feet.' I don't think that this is lucrative in and of itself. It's because of being interviewed that people seek me for this.*

FROM BLACK FEMME DOMMING & THE ART OF REPARATIONS WITH MISTRESS VELVET (VOLUME III)

While they're not a requirement, niches can be helpful for many, especially those who struggle to define their brand or find the right clients. Niches can vary from clip store categories and kink markets, to certain characteristics you embody. It is important to recognize that you may intentionally play into some niches, and other niches will be thrust upon you. It is up to you if you want to embrace them, profit off of them, or create your own!

> *I don't care where you go on the planet. If you're brand fucking new, somebody is gonna want to fuck with you.*

FROM NICHE MARKETING WITH MIA DARQUE (VOLUME VI)

Niches can be broken into three categories: the way you present (tall, short, pregnant, hair color, etc), who you are (race, ethnicity, sex assigned at birth), and what you do (activities, styles, demeanor).

To start, fill out the rest of this chart with words to describe each associated category. You can always go back and change it. Our niches don't have to be stagnant. After you fill out the chart, you can decide and circle the characteristics or words that feel good to market or incorporate into your brand and/or niche. None of the columns have to relate to one another. Circle any word from any column that feels good to you. We've provided a few examples so you can get the hang of it!

NICHES		
What I Look Like	**Who I Am**	**What I do**
Bald BBW	Jewish Trans	Elaborate Roleplays Corporal Punishment

Take it from Mistress Mia Darque in her talk **Niche Marketing (Volume VI)**: *"I've never seen something as sad as a person who was trying their damnedest and not making any traction in any way in what they're trying to do. When something as simple as paying attention to your surroundings could be one of the quickest fixes. Try selling something else. Stop giving them what we want. Give them what they need. You can find your own group, you can have your own thing, if you're willing to put in that work."*

If you're finding yourself running into a wall repeatedly trying to find clients to no avail or you're continuously fetishized or approached for a niche you *don't* want to engage in, choosing your own niche can help you control the conversation. A niche makes the fantasy less about *you* and more about *what you're doing*. You could be great, but when you're wearing latex, or putting them in a diaper, it's more about the love of the game than submitting to you specifically. This can be especially helpful if you find one or more of your identities is being fetishized, i.e. the niche is thrust upon you. Control the conversation by appealing to a market where who you are doesn't matter, it is more about what you do. Your niche clients are more likely to be in the fetishist category, given the nature of the niche.

Everyone uses niches differently. This is a *very small* sampling of a few different pros, and how niches fit into their brand (or not):

Ariana Chevalier, largely considered the best in the world regarding latex fetish, started down her rubbery path because the first house she worked in, she was told because of her skin color, she wouldn't make as much money as the white Dommes. What started with one of her clients buying her rubber grew into an entire specialty. She now is a household name in the latex world and proved that first house wrong.

Daddy An Li is very well known for whips, CBT, and domestic service. She does not market herself as "The Whipping Domme," "The CBT Goblin" or "The Queen of Servitude." All of her niches fit well into her overall brand.

Lola Jean operates within the wrestling niche. All of the clients she sees are wrestling related, and she does not take any sessions that veer out of this market. She also only operates on the wrestling fetish website and not other BDSM directories or ad sites.

Mistress Shayla found herself in the niche of FTT, and she liked it...for a while. Niches can become mundane over time, and she has worked to pivot herself into other activities she enjoys, like medfet and caning.

Empress Wu is well known for blood play and off-the-wall roleplay. If you are familiar with NYC you know that there is no shortage of blood thirsty Dom/me/mxs over here. It's a never ending supply of vampires. Wu is not into blood play to take advantage of a niche. She's into it because she loves blood, and because she's good at it.

Oran Julius' speciality is all types of breath play. They teach classes in mummification, bagging, waterboarding, etc, and also have a variety of clips and porn featuring these topics. While they don't actively promote or highlight these niches, it is fairly obvious because of how much of their content is in these categories.

Everyone wants to be known for this one thing well, but don't pigeonhole yourself. Don't just look at one niche. Look at niche adjacent things. Blackmail fantasy is a niche I fell into. So, If you are into blackmail fantasy, then what else are you typically into?

FROM MAKING ANALYTICS YOUR BITCH WITH AMBERLY ROTHFIELD (VOLUME VI)

ONLINE NICHES & UNDERSERVED MARKETS

Finding an underrepresented niche can be helpful to find a category with low supply (and, potentially, high demand). A great way to start this search is by looking online.

Pick the niches that you want to dominate first by scoping out what, who, and how much is already out there in that niche. You're not doing this to copy exactly what others do. You're doing this to see the type, quality, content, etc. that is already available and then try to fill in the holes. Maybe your angle has to do with the way you look, your demeanor, or the type of session you offer within that niche. Use what you have to differentiate yourself and let potential clients know why you are unique within this area.

It can be helpful to think of specialized skills to influence the underserved markets, i.e., how many people are capable of lactating, or skilled in wrestling? Then, of those, how many are actually offering this as a service within their domination? Is there an opportunity to create a new market or category based on the skills or qualities you possess? Look into niche-adjacent markets. Finding one niche can lead you down a rabbit hole to many niches! While it's not a foolproof equation, it can often tell you what markets could be worth investing in.

PRO TIP

A niche is something *very specific*, not something within a larger group. If you're into medfet, while that can be a specialty...it's not a niche. "Extraterrestrial Domme who kidnaps humans and does depraved experiments on their trembling bodies" definitely is.

WHAT IF THERE ARE OTHER PEOPLE IN YOUR NICHE?

Great! This is a wonderful opportunity. Don't see them as competition, but as comrades. Figure out ways to work with them and support them. Can you create content together? Offer double sessions? Their clients and your clients will often have a bit of a crossover, and a great working relationship can often have results greater than the sum of its parts.

CONSEQUENCES OF SOME NICHES (WHEN THE NICHE CHOOSES YOU)

When your niche falls into the *way you present* or *who you are* categories, you may find that a niche is thrust upon you without choosing to exploit this of your own volition. Just because you naturally have qualities of a certain niche does *not* mean you have to monetize, act on, or address this in any of your work if you don't want to. Especially with racial, religious, or gender-based niches that may have a lot of baggage and trauma inherent in this play and/or identity fetishization.

> *You have to make that choice if you're going to give in and play along with the racism that you experience in order to get that coin, or if you're going to let those folks go. That's a decision that I grapple with. Sometimes, I'm in a place financially, emotionally, and physically, where I can let that person go, and it's fine. And sometimes, I need whoever comes my way.*

FROM BLACK FEMME DOMMING & THE ART OF REPARATIONS WITH MISTRESS VELVET (VOLUME III)

BRAND IDENTITY & YOUR NICHE

When you want to do more of a certain type of session or establish yourself in a niche, you need to present it. This is your brand marketing. This is different from your brand identity, which is the voice you use in your brand marketing. If you are still shaping your brand identity, sometimes finding your niche can help you foster that. On the flip side, be wary of making your entire brand identity your niche, in the event you want to move out of that niche or reinvent your practice.

> *If you want to start doing a certain activity more with clients, start advertising for it. Talk about it. Use standard marketing techniques because that's how I did it. You talk about it, you put it on your website, you do all these things to market yourself for it.*

FROM THE PSYCHOLOGY OF A TOILET WITH DADDY AN LI (VOLUME 7)

Example: Daddy An Li loves shit sessions. She wants to do more shit sessions. Instead of waiting for clients to request shit sessions with her, Daddy An Li proceeds to talk about how much she loves shitting on Twitter, on blog posts on her websites, and in clips. This is Daddy An Li's brand marketing. Her brand identity is both her persona as a Pro Bully and a style of sensual and strict sadism.

Example: Lola Jean wants to operate in the niche market of fetish wrestling. Lola Jean uses her brand marketing by promoting herself exclusively as such and listing her ad on fetish wrestling websites. Her brand identity is being cocky, strong, and condescending.

SKILL SETS

There are generally two routes when it comes to attracting clientele. Either the client seeks you out because you are whatever makes you, you. Or they seek you out because of the things that you do. Or maybe both!

The number of potential skills for you to master may seem overwhelming. From CBT to hypnosis to medical play, there is plenty for you to get your hands dirty. While there is nothing wrong with trying a bit of everything to see what you like, you don't have to know how to *do* everything. Hell, there is not enough time in the day to be an expert at it all.

JACK OF ALL TRADES, MASTER OF NONE

You don't need to know how to execute every single skill. It is not feasible. You can always start with a few skills or activities, and build off of those once you have a handle on them. Biting off more than you can chew can be tempting (and we love your tenacity!) but slow growth is much more sustainable, and affords you the time and resources to learn even more.

BIG FISH IN A SMALL POND

If you are a lone provider in a market, i.e. the one of the few providers in Scotland, the only Dom/me/mx in a 100 mile distance in the Dakotas, etc., you have the benefit of being the first person people will see in that area. You don't have to focus as hard on a niche unless you exclusively want to perform actions in that niche. You are the only oasis for miles around, enjoy it.

HOW WILL I KNOW WHEN I'M READY TO BRING A NEW SKILL INTO SESSION?

The truth is, there is no consensus on when someone is "officially" ready to add the skill to their list of potential activities. There is never a right time. It depends on your risk profile, the level of risk of the activity, and how much practice you've had. This is all relative.

IN SUMMARY

1. A niche can create a new market when you're not finding success with the current one.
2. You don't need a niche to be successful.
3. Don't let a niche that chose you keep you from pursuing what you really want to do in your practice.

CHAPTER 13: PERSONAS, STYLES, NICHES

Have good work boundaries! That starts with what parts of yourself you want to bring into your practice and what you want to keep for just you.

WHAT DOES MY PERSONA FEEL LIKE? WHAT ARE THE DEFINING CHARACTERISTICS AND QUALITIES?

WHAT PHYSICAL CHARACTERISTICS SET ME APART? DO I WANT TO PLAY WITH THESE IN MY MARKETING OR KEEP THESE FOR MYSELF?

IS MY "WORK" PERSONA DIFFERENT FROM MY REAL LIFE PERSONA? WHAT QUALITIES ARE DIFFERENT?

WHAT ARE SOME POSSIBLE NICHES I COULD FIT INTO?

DOES MY PERSONA CHANGE BASED ON THE PERSON OR ACTIVITY?

DOES IT FEEL DRAINING OR CHALLENGING TO STAY IN MY WORK PERSONA FOR LONGER PERIODS?

WHAT EXPERIENCE DO YOU PROVIDE OR WANT TO PROVIDE?

HOMEWORK

Write an eulogy about your persona or each of them if there is more than one. Describe their best qualities.

HOMEWORK

Dearly beloved, we are gathered here today to celebrate the life of:

CHAPTER 14
SOCIAL MEDIA

You don't need to be present on every social media platform, especially if you're just starting out. Focus on the ones that feel manageable for you and then add to those when it feels appropriate. At minimum, we would suggest having a Twitter, as this is the best platform to connect with other Dominants and build community. It is also (as of this writing) one of the more lenient platforms, but each social media platform and its Terms of Service changes so regularly, we'd have to put out a new edition every month to keep up. Marketing platforms are *endless*. What you can and cannot advertise varies by platform (thanks SESTA/FOSTA). Advertising platforms vary wildly between cities and countries and get seized all the time.

SOCIAL MEDIA

We could write an entire book on how to use social media for advertising. But, then again, social media and its algorithms are constantly changing so it would become irrelevant upon publishing. Social media can be helpful and it can also be a big drain on your energy. It's important to have at least a few "official" accounts– Instagram, Twitter, Fetlife. This gives you something called *social proof*.

Social proof essentially means you exist– that you're a person who actively exists on the internet in some capacity, rather than just an ad that may be fake, or a phone sex listing using stolen or bought photos. These "official" accounts will also allow you to network with other sex workers, and having a network is invaluable to your long-term practice.

PRO TIP

The best way to connect with providers in your area is to check out your ad sites and many will have links to each provider's social media. If you're in the middle of nowhere and don't know anyone else, you'll still have the social media handles of the folks around you to get started.

It's easy to get FOMO or imposter syndrome using social media. You have hundreds of thousands of photos and videos of incredible Dominants doing their thing; how on earth will you stand out? What does your brand voice sound like? Take some of the writing exercises from earlier and rewrite them as captions or tweets. What is the general vibe of your copy? Is it irreverent or silly? Stern? Educational? Mom-like?

WHAT ARE SOME BUZZWORDS I CAN USE TO DESCRIBE MY SOCIAL MEDIA PRESENCE?

It's important to note that social media should NOT be used to directly solicit clients, as this is against many of the services' ToS and can get you booted. We use social media as a call to action: promoting fansites, tours, and session ideas we want to manifest in our practice. Throwing up a tame photo of a new outfit you've got and captioning it "this corset is amazing, and only my subscribers get to see it" can inspire someone to buy your content. An announcement that you're spending two days in another city and offering sessions can inspire a far-flung admirer to finally book with you. A tweet thread describing one of your favorite kinky moments may resonate with someone enough to convince them to reach out for a booking.

DISCOURSE, DRAMA, AND DISCOURAGEMENT

If you spend just 15 minutes browsing any form of social media, you'll probably experience three things: someone arguing a point you don't agree with, someone posting gossip (or worse, "vaguebooking"), and a photo or video of someone's vacation/shopping haul/other thing that you want but someone else has. It gets to be a lot after a while. Maybe you indulge a little longer, arguing your point with an internet stranger who doesn't listen. Or you feel bad looking at a friend's expensive new boots, thinking there's something wrong with you for not getting the same treatment.

There's a simple answer here: social media is a lie. All of it. We will simply work with the assumption that everything posted to Facebook/Twitter/Instagram is trying to sell you something, and since we are also here to sell something (our professional services) we will not be swayed by other people's marketing. Someone's written a thread about how they hate when Pros do XYZ? Ignore it. Someone's posted about their FMTY (fly me to you) to a fancy hotel in the Maldives? Ignore it. Someone who posts about how they hate other people is someone who secretly hates themselves a little bit, or maybe just has bad boundaries about what they should share on social media. Someone who posts constantly about their gifts could have purchased it themselves and pretended it was a gift to inspire clients. The easiest way to do social media is to treat it like everyone is an actor in a play. We're all saying our lines and playing our parts, in order to get the audience to believe our stories.

PRO TIP
STAYING SANE ON THE INTERNET
1. Limit scrolling to less than 15 mins per day
2. Remember everything is a lie
3. Do not feed the trolls
4. Use the block and mute buttons religiously
5. If you get irritated at something/someone, it's time to log off

SOCIAL MEDIA AS NETWORKING

Social media is a great way to get to know other industry folks. You'll be exposed to classes, discourse, and extremely cool media from some extremely cool folks. Following other pros and regularly interacting with their posts can be a great way to make friends, learn something new, and get inspired to create something cool on your own. Look for accounts local to your area and reach out to see if there are any meetups or parties happening. Never underestimate the power of an IRL meeting. Some of the best clients have been introduced to a Dom/me/mx at a party or a class. Frequenting BDSM nights in your area can be a great way to network with others. Never solicit directly, this is not only a bad idea, but disrespectful to the party hosts. But being "known" in your local scene means word of mouth, which is when others do your advertising for you.

ONLINE PERSONA

If the way you present yourself online is significantly different than how you present in person, you may find some clients struggling with this. They likely have a fantasy version of you in their head. You get to decide how much you try to cater to that fantasy, but if there is a big difference, you might need to win them over to the IRL version of you to replace that fantasy.

PRO TIP

Are you stern, cold, and high protocol online, but warm, giggly, and sweet in session? Try to match your online voice with your in-person voice, so it resonates with the right people.

CLARITY AROUND FULL SERVICE

For a number of reasons, you may be vague in online spaces about whether or not you offer full service. Vagueness breeds opportunities for assumptions and miscommunication, so you may end up with a client expecting something you weren't prepared to offer. After (and only after) you've verified someone and ruled them out as someone safe to have intimate conversations with, make sure you are clear about what is and is not on the table in your sessions.

IN SUMMARY

1. Social media is important, but it's not the end of the world.
2. Your social media is client-facing. It's a marketing tool to show clients you're real and you're someone they want to book.
3. Discourse is anathema to what you're using SW Twitter for.
4. Avoid the endless scroll that takes focus off you & your practice.

CHAPTER 14: SOCIAL MEDIA

Social media can easily become a time suck. Set your structure now so you can keep your eyes on the prize and use your time appropriately.

WHAT WILL BE MY MAIN PURPOSE OR GOAL WITH SOCIAL MEDIA? TO CONNECT WITH COMMUNITY? TO GET CLIENTS?

HOW WILL I USE SOCIAL MEDIA?

WILL I HAVE A DIFFERENT STRATEGY FOR EACH PLATFORM?

HOW WILL I MEASURE SUCCESS BASED ON MY MAIN GOALS OF SOCIAL MEDIA?

HOW MUCH TIME IS REALISTIC TO SPEND ON EACH PLATFORM?

HOMEWORK

Make a Twitter handle. It doesn't matter what your name is, you can change it later. Follow 10 people (ideally in your area) and at least 10 other people that they follow.

CHAPTER 15
CULTURE & ETIQUETTE

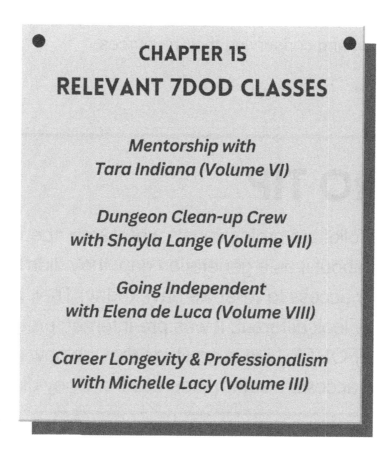

CHAPTER 15
RELEVANT 7DOD CLASSES

*Mentorship with
Tara Indiana (Volume VI)*

*Dungeon Clean-up Crew
with Shayla Lange (Volume VII)*

*Going Independent
with Elena de Luca (Volume VIII)*

*Career Longevity & Professionalism
with Michelle Lacy (Volume III)*

Remember when we told you at the very beginning of the workbook that community is everything? Well, this is how you maintain it. Because we are in an unregulated industry, community is what regulates us. This has its ups and downs, but ultimately highlights the importance of being in community and not only existing in a silo.

Community keeps us safe, and can also make us successful. But you can't just show up and demand community. You will only get out of it what you put into it. Don't feel that you have to earn your stripes in order to eat at the table, but realize that this industry has immense turnover. Some individuals (clients and colleagues alike) have been burned or taken advantage of by tourist Dominants who think this career is an easy cash grab they can pop in and out of whenever they want.

Much like clients, seasoned Dominants are choosy when selecting where they want to put their energy, time, or resources. Do not take offense if that Dom/me/mx you admire online doesn't immediately jump to have coffee with you and offer their advice. If you're patient, you make a true effort, and you stick around long enough to prove you're not a tourist (and we know you're not, because you bought this workbook), they will come around. It is not a reflection of you and who you are, it is an act of self-protection and conserving their resources.

PRO TIP

Old Guard folks are professionals who came about at an earlier time. Think about it as a generation gap: they didn't have the resources or access to what we have today. Their professional practice may look different. It was pre-internet, pre-clipsites, pre-SESTA/FOSTA. Live in gratitude that we now have more options and access to safer resources than they did.

DO Learn about the whores who came before you.

DON'T Rip copy and content directly from other Dominants.

DO Offer trade or compensation when asking for someone's time and energy.

DON'T Act entitled to another Dom/me/mx's time, space, or expertise.

DO Answer reference requests and say thank you after an answered request.

DON'T Shit talk other Dom/me/mxs to clients.

DO Claim your wins, but constantly bragging just screams insecurity.

DON'T Let clients see or access blacklists or bad date lists.

We want you to be safe, successful, and fulfilled. For most in this industry, finding a balance between those three takes time. Be kind and patient to yourself so you can figure out what this looks like for you.

PRO TIP

Sometimes there is tension or dissonance between new and old guard. If you ever suffer weirdness from the old guard, don't sweat it. It's not personal, and not necessarily gatekeeping. It's like an unfortunate trauma response that no one is happy about.

BUILDING SOCIAL PROOF

Social proof is the idea that you exist as a real human and not just a catfish on the internet. Social proof is built through social media, your website, and your network. Attending kink events, sex work organization fundraisers, etc. are good ways to show face and build proof, not to mention building your network or finding new doubles partners.

We recommend you have at least two social media profiles in addition to your website. Fetlife, Twitter, Instagram, Tiktok, and Reddit are all platforms that can do wonders for your social proof. It doesn't mean you have to use it religiously, but it should exist. Photos, whether candid or professional, text posts, polls, comments/RTs, etc., show people you are an independent mind and not just three scambots in a trenchcoat.

Even better is when other professionals follow or interact with you. Clients see this and it eases their mind. If you can be trusted by other verified professionals, you can probably be trusted by the client.

IN SUMMARY

1. Be friendly. Be polite. Be someone others want to be around.
2. Learn how other people and spaces operate.
3. Making connections in this industry does not happen overnight, but over time you can make lifelong friends.

CHAPTER 15: CULTURE AND ETIQUETTE

Community is everything, no matter where you are.
How will you foster or build yours?

HOW WILL I DEVELOP RELATIONSHIPS OR FRIENDSHIPS WITH OTHER WORKERS IN MY AREA?

HOW WILL I DEVELOP RELATIONSHIPS OR FRIENDSHIPS WITH OTHER WORKERS ONLINE?

ARE THERE ANY LOCAL EVENTS OR GATHERINGS I CAN GO TO WHERE I CAN MEET OTHER WORKERS?

HOMEWORK

Find and attend a community event, whether a party, a gathering or an online meetup.

What are you going to wear?

CHAPTER 16
PUBLICITY

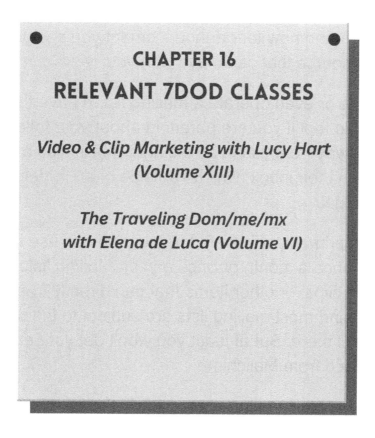

Just like social media and additional sources of income, you don't need *all* of these to be successful. Pick and choose what feels manageable and sustainable, then add from there if needed.

DON'T SWEAT THE SMALL STUFF

Followers, subscribers, stans, and fans will come and go. Sometimes it affects your bottom line, and sometimes it just means the number at the end of your follower count is a bit lower than it was yesterday. While tracking analytics can be helpful, you shouldn't live and die by them. Sometimes losing ten followers may be because they deactivated their account, they were all bots to begin with, or the wind was blowing slightly northwest. Everything doesn't *have* to mean something, but it may be worth noting if it is part of a larger trend.

THE UTILITY OF AN EMAIL LIST

Accounts are being seized by our social media overlords on a regular basis, and even if you can retain them, relying on the everchanging algorithm to deliver the information you want to the people you want can be a roll of the dice. To safeguard any potential social shutdowns, loss of your growing following, and/or your followers not getting to see that brand new tour announcement you spent valuable time making, you need a resource that can move with you.

You don't *have* to utilize or even operate a mailing list to have the practice you want. However, it is a valuable tool if you are paranoid about your following and/or online contacts being taken away from you in an instant. This is also a method to get yourself wedged right in their inbox, which– outside of an in-person meet and greet– is as direct as you can get!

Having a mailing list is primarily a failsafe for you. You can use it as little or as often as you want, whether once a month or once a year. Mailing lists can be fruitful when announcing tours, new clips, or other items that can directly translate to money in your pocket. Keep in mind most mailing lists are subject to the same ToS as social media, so the risk is still there. But at least you won't get your email list snatched even if you do get booted from Mailchimp.

Only plan on using email blasts to say things like "Mistress Coffeecup is coming to Chicago March 4-6th. Get an early bird rate if you pre-book today." You want to keep the information as concise and vague as possible.

GROWING YOUR MAILING LIST

Asking individuals to sign up for your mailing list on social media sometimes feels like screaming into the void. It is also not the only way to grow your mailing list. You can take a carrot dangling approach, such as offering a free clip upon signup, or you can manually add anyone who fills out your intake form or sends an email to your mailing list. Once you find it worth the investment, you can use third party apps to automate mailing list signups upon certain actions.

Not all email marketing companies are whore-friendly. In fact, most of them aren't, so you'll still have to manage some of what you say, but not to the same extent as you do on Instagram or TikTok.

Consider when choosing a mailing list provider:

- ★ Do you pay per user, per email, or flat fee?
- ★ Are there existing templates you can use?
- ★ When asked for your address be sure to use one you're okay with being easily searchable. Try a PO Box or mail forwarding service.
- ★ Are there easy integrations to collect email via other functions besides manually?

LINK AGGREGATORS

Link aggregators (like Linktree, allmylinks etc.) can be wonderful tools to house your many different points of sale and avenues to contact you, especially if you don't have a website. This is where you can house links to your fan sites, session inquiry forms, Sext panther, Niteflirt, and even podcast appearances. Link aggregators can also be a replacement for a standalone website, or at least buy you time until you make one!

While these are incredibly useful, they are not impervious to FOSTA/SESTA either. Many will boot you for housing or mentioning fan sites, per their terms of service. Regularly check any links or link aggregators to make sure they are still active. When in doubt, you can always create a splash page on your website or a quick one-page site with a variety of buttons that mimic a Linktree but lead the user towards your preferred platforms.

Be wary of where you post these. With the ever-changing terms of service in a post SESTA/FOSTA landscape, what was okay last month might be a red flag today. Pay attention to your ads and fansites; many don't let you link out to booking forms or websites other than theirs.

PRO TIP

Tour a location more than once to build momentum. Nothing is more annoying than someone contacting you the moment your tour is over asking to book with you. Follow up with "You've just missed me but I'll be back in the fall/spring/whenever here's the link to my mailing list to keep up to date with my tour schedule" can be the difference between your next tour being awesome or a bust.

MAKING A MARKETING SUITE

Contributed by Mia Darque

You don't have to save up for a fancy photoshoot or have the nicest corset or the fiercest nails when you start out. Everyone needs a tool belt, and an editing suite on your phone could be yours.

We recommend starting with these apps, or something comparable:

- ★ **YouCut - Video Editor V Recorder**
- ★ **Video Splitter**
- ★ **Video Watermark**
- ★ **Meme Generator**
- ★ **Remove.bg**
- ★ **Canva**
- ★ **Send Anywhere Inshot**

Most of these apps have a free/limited version, but upgrading to the pro versions are less than $10 apiece (with the exception of canva, at $120 a year). Maybe it means cooking more from home or doing your own pedicure instead of a professional one, but try to find a way to scrape together these tools to benefit your business, and they will pay you back tenfold.

NONTRADITIONAL ADVERTISING

You will use many tools in the pursuit of your career, whether it be your social media presence, advertising dollars, or face-to-face interactions. None of these three supersedes the other. It will depend on your preference and where your target market finds you. It may seem like social media and ads are the only way to market, but this is because they are the most visible. There are other, less traditional routes to getting your name out there.

Long before there was the internet, professional Dominants had to shake hands and greet new faces to push and promote themselves. This might look like writing the name of your website on the bathroom mirror at the bar or showing face at local community events. You can get as guerrilla as you want with it, but also think of what clientele you want to target. Where do they frequent? How will they find you?

In addition to your online strategy, don't underestimate the offline ones. While free advertising isn't always amazing, it does work. It just requires more filtering of the requests that you receive from it.

What are three types of face-to-face or non-traditional promotion that you're comfortable with?

TOURING AS ADVERTISING

You may see a lot of your favorite pros announcing tours on their Twitter accounts. While touring can seem overwhelming, and there is certainly an amount of financial risk involved, it can also be beneficial if your current market isn't cutting it. This might be because you live in a small town, or you want to see how different parts of the world respond to your look or your niche. Maybe California isn't into BBWs but Iowa can't get enough. Amazons might feel like a lackluster market in Texas but there's more demand than supply in Canada (these are not facts, we just made them up).

PRO TIP

Tour a location more than once to build momentum. Nothing is more annoying than someone contacting you the moment your tour is over asking to book with you. Follow up with "You've just missed me but I'll be back in the fall/spring/whenever here's the link to my mailing list to keep up to date with my tour schedule" can be the difference between your next tour being awesome or a bust.

There's a lot of overhead to think about before testing the waters, so don't be afraid to start small. Travel to a different city in your state/region instead of hopping on a plane. Do a day trip instead of an overnight. Tour with others to save costs on the space, Ubers, and potentially pooling resources like toys and tools.

If you are touring and using public play spaces or local dungeons, make sure that you are getting them involved in your marketing, if possible, because they likely already have patrons and followers who would love to know about new or exclusive professionals coming to the space. This is a way for you to be a flavor of the month or get "new person money" even if you're more established in your career.

IN SUMMARY

There are a million inexpensive and/or free ways to put yourself out there. Maintaining connections with the world outside your immediate area, both on and offline can help get your practice off the ground.

CHAPTER 16: PUBLICITY

Social media isn't the only thing you can use to set your nets. How will people find out about you? Do you want to be found?

WHAT IS MY PRIMARY GOAL OF MY ONLINE CONTENT? TO MAKE MONEY? ATTRACT CLIENTS?

WHAT'S MY POLICY ON TALKING TO MEDIA SUCH AS PODCASTS?

THREE FORMS OF NON-TRADITIONAL AND/OR UNPAID ADVERTISING I CAN USE:

HOW WILL I ORGANIZE ALL OF THE WAYS PEOPLE CAN GIVE ME MONEY?

HOMEWORK

Make a link aggregator. Populate it with every platform where people can find you.

CHAPTER 17

MAINTAINING CLIENT RELATIONSHIPS

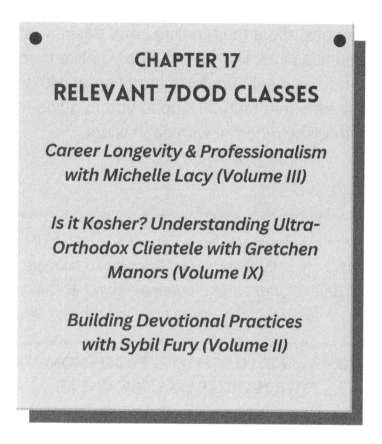

IDENTIFYING WHAT YOUR CLIENT NEEDS

Everyone's got a favorite client. Perhaps they're your favorite because you've got chemistry in session or they know what gift to get you at the right time. Maybe they communicate in a style that feels good to you, maybe they follow even the strictest protocol you lay out. Whatever the reason– maybe you want more sessions you enjoy, or for the reliable income– if they aren't already, you may wish they were more of a regular.

Regulars come in all types. Some weekly, some monthly, some a few times a year. We want every new client we see to become a regular, and we can only do that by understanding what they need. This is more than just their in-session desires. It's about the role that YOU play in fulfilling their needs.

Perhaps the client feels you serve a therapeutic role. Perhaps they feel you are more of a disciplinarian. Maybe you make them feel young again, or make them feel important and confident. They can't always articulate how you make them feel, but if you can hit the right combination of feeling buttons, they'll return again and again.

Similar to love languages and attachment styles, you can figure out what they need and want by how they speak about their feelings and desires. Asking questions like "what does your ideal session look like" or "how do you like to feel" can help you gather their thoughts and desires. Many folks aren't great with their own feelings–they can't identify, let alone name them. It's up to you to guide them through this process. Your approach will be different with each client.

 There are the clients looking for a connection with that one special person that really gets them and that's going to be a chunk of your business. Then other ones who bounce around will always bounce around back to you--and at some point a large amount of them.

FROM CAREER LONGEVITY & PROFESSIONALISM WITH MICHELLE LACY (VOLUME III)

The Thank You Email

Never underestimate the power of a good thank you email after a session. Clients sometimes have "post nut clarity" after a scene, or feelings of shame, fatigue, low moods, etc. This is common knowledge in the lifestyle world; many people plan for and acknowledge *sub drop*, but clients often don't have a game plan for the ups and downs that can come after seeing a professional.

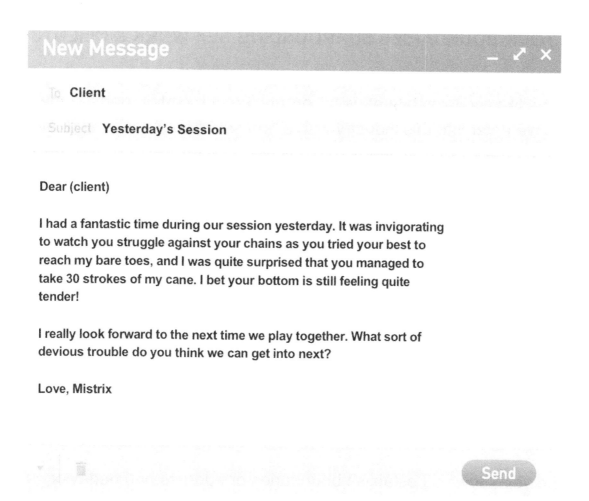

This email tells the client a few key things:

★ They aren't the horrible, depraved pervert they think they are.
★ Another human has witnessed their shame and not even batted an eyelash.
★ You had a great time.
★ You would be willing to see them again.

Leaning into your favorite parts of the session invites the client to share with you what they loved most. This gives you an insight into their psyche, what they value, what they cherish in a scene. It also gives you great feedback and fodder for a testimonials page on your website.

In addition, you can use your email signature to corral all your links together like on your aggregator pages. You can list your wishlists, your phone/cam sites, clip sites and fansites in the signature— any way for your clients to say thank you in a way that is much more tangible than just an email back.

FINDING YOUR BOUNDARIES SURROUNDING SEX WORK & CLIENTS

We've already established that boundaries are important things to have. Boundaries can be things like "no texts late at night" or "don't touch certain parts of my body." Sometimes we enter into this industry with a firm set of boundaries and, over time, we let others cross them for various reasons. Maybe your no touching rule changes when the client is a whale. Maybe the no texts boundary is relaxed for your favorite client. Maybe you run into a boundary you didn't even know you had. If something feels icky, uncomfortable, or leaves you feeling bummed afterwards, you *do not* have to keep doing it. Anyone who tells you that you *have* to do things you're uncomfortable with is an asshole.

Revisiting boundaries over time is important. Boundaries can and do change as you spend more time in the industry. Regularly writing down and examining your boundaries helps you be intentional in setting and enforcing them, rather than just letting them go by the wayside. Boundaries can move in two directions– tighter and looser. Acknowledging each boundary change helps you move confidently and assertively through each interaction with clients.

In the same vein, how you establish boundaries or address bad behavior can vary between clients. Someone who sees you as a disciplinarian might appreciate a spanking for bad behavior, whereas a brat who sees you as a challenge would love it and misbehave over and over as a fun game. Someone who sees you as a confidant might feel hurt or unwanted if you don't also share emotional intimacy or secrets with them, but would relish in mimicking the intimacy by having a "dirty little secret" between the two of you.

PRO TIP

Do kink in your personal life? Set boundaries around the kinks you engage in with clients. Whether it's saving "missionary" style pegging for your partners, relegating an honorific to loved ones only, or simply not offering certain services for pay, it's a great way to keep your personal play from feeling too much like "work."

CHANGING YOUR BOUNDARIES WITH CLIENTS

Perhaps you've got a longtime regular who you let text you sometimes, but now it's annoying the crap out of you. Or a client who you let profess their undying love for you, but now they're getting a divorce and actually think they're going to be able to date you off the clock.

You have a few strategies for changing the boundaries with a client. Please note none of these are foolproof, some clients won't take well to being told no, and they may wander off to find someone who does tolerate whatever behavior you won't. This is ultimately a good thing– losing a client who annoys the shit out of you with their bad/overstepping behavior frees up emotional energy for you to find new ones who behave much better.

Eroticize the boundaries: perhaps you have a client who gets quite handsy when they're turned on. All the blood rushes out of the critical thinking part of their brain and the little head does the thinking. The little head has notoriously bad judgment. Convince the little head that it's hotter if you get your way. "You desire me so badly that you can't stop trying to touch, I'm going to move just out of your way so you feel nothing but suffering as I get to caress all the most delicate parts of me that you crave."

Bring feelings into it: maybe you have a client that tries to haggle. He saw you when you were newer, or had lower rates than you do now, and expects preferential treatment. "It hurts my feelings that you see my worth as less than my hottie friends. You and I have built something so wonderful together, I would hate to let that all go to waste."

Upsell: a client texts you with pornographic fantasies, and you're annoyed with it. Tell them you'd love to respond to this with depraved fantasies of your own, but the phone they're currently texting can sometimes be seen by a sister/a nephew/a nosy vanilla boss/etc. Have them send those texts via Niteflirt or Sext Panther, where you can respond with steamy messages and photos, safe from prying eyes.

Physically restrain them: client talking shit or trying to stick their tongue out? Gag 'em. Roving hands? Cuff 'em. Trying to lift up to eat booty during FTT? Set the toilet chair to the highest setting, so all they can do is lie and wait.

When in doubt, roll back slowly. Maybe it's your most valuable regular, and if you stopped seeing them it would put you in a financially precarious position. Take longer to respond to their texts outside of business hours. Try more bondage and blindfolds. Carrot dangle what they want in exchange for good behavior. You can't force them to behave better instantly, but you can play defensively against their most annoying tendencies. This will buy you time to formulate a game plan to enact any of the steps listed above, or work on replacing the most annoying or irredeemable clientele with new ones.

TRANSITIONING ONLINE CLIENTS TO IRL

Contributed by Oran Julius

Marketing yourself online can be different from how you show up in person and that's okay! There are many benefits to presenting yourself one way online, even if it's not exactly how you show up in person, including:

Leaning on fantasies: Online presence is all marketing, and the goal is to get them to open their wallet. Once they do, you can charm them however you feel will work best, but getting them in the door initially may require relying on some tried and true fantasies.

Separation: Some of us need separation between our online and IRL personas in order for this work to feel sustainable. Create space for you to be a you that can be maintained.

Authenticity: For some of us, crafting an online image is easier than performing an IRL one. For others, it's the opposite. Regardless of which comes more naturally to you, allowing yourself to not have to be exactly the same online and IRL will induce less stress and allow you to be more authentic in both worlds.

Surprises keep them coming back: I can't count how many times I've been told that my online persona scared clients and they found me much more approachable IRL. Showing them another side of you can be a pleasant surprise and make them feel connected to you in a way that keeps them hooked.

Variety: Especially in the online world, getting to exhibit different personas allows you to provide variety to the same clients, or reach a few different pools of clients.

Niteflirt is a great place to take advantage of this, through creating multiple ads that hit on different sides of you.

> **IN SUMMARY**
> 1. If you don't know what the client needs from you, you can't continue to fulfill those needs.
> 2. Set boundaries early and often. It's easier to set a boundary up front than have to walk it back later on.
> 3. Create separation between work you and private you, lest things feel muddled or crappy.

CHAPTER 17: MAINTAINING CLIENT RELATIONSHIPS

Regulars are an important part of the business. Understand the life cycle of your ongoing client relationships with these questions.

WHAT DISTINGUISHES A CLIENT WHO GETS PRIVILEGES FROM ONE WHO DOESN'T?

CURRENT BOUNDARIES I HAVE WITH EVERY CLIENT

BOUNDARIES I HAVE WITH SOME CLIENTS

> WHAT ARCHETYPES DO MY CLIENTS HAVE? ARE THEY ALL SAD BOYS? BROS? DIVORCED?

> HOW CAN I TAILOR SESSIONS & COMMUNICATION TO GENERATE REPEAT BUSINESS WITHOUT CHANGING WHO I AM?

WHAT NEED(S) DO I FILL IN MY POTENTIAL OR CURRENT CLIENT'S LIFE?

WHAT CAN I DO TO ENCOURAGE THOSE BONDS?

WHAT DYNAMICS DO I WANT TO FOSTER WITH MY CLIENTELE?

IF I'VE LET SOMEONE GET TOO COMFORTABLE, HOW WILL I REASSERT MY BOUNDARIES?

HOMEWORK

Create a sample follow-up email where you can fill in specifics unique to each client, like a kinky Mad Lib.

CHAPTER 18
CASH FLOW POST SESSION

> **CHAPTER 18**
> **RELEVANT 7DOD CLASSES**
>
> *Sensual FinDom with Faustine Cox (Volume IV)*
>
> *Multiple Income Streams (Volume IV) with Jet Setting Jasmine*
>
> *Making Analytics Your Bitch with Amberly Rothfield (Volume VI)*

Whether you do online or in-person work, there's always more money to be made. Your clients want to support you, but might not always be the whales you dream of keeping in the stable. There are many different ways to make money, both active and passive. Your active income is the money you get from things you have to do each time, like sessioning, camming, or selling used socks. Passive income is when something you've made can be continuously sold, long after the work is done. These are items like clips, fansites, or wishlists.

If your first thought is holy shit, I don't want six other jobs, relax. This is not about you doing more work, it's more about working smarter and seeing how we may be leaving a stream of income on the table already.

MULTIPLE INCOME STREAMS WITH JET SETTING JASMINE (VOLUME IV)

Diversify your income. Putting all your eggs in one basket is never a good idea. Fansites disappear, advertising platforms get seized by the FBI, health issues can prevent us from working in person, or we may just straight up get sick of doing what we're doing.

It's also important to diversify your price points. An IRL worker generally has a minimum spend where x amount of time = x amount of cash, and usually it isn't cheap. While we don't want to water ourselves down for the cheapest clients, we *do* want a range of price points, so even the most cash-strapped client feels they can still participate in the fantasy. Spending $5-$100 is well within the budget for most folks. And if that $5 or $25 or $100 is made without you even lifting a finger? Even better.

You want to make it as easy as possible for them to spend money on you. This applies to online work, too. Someone who calls you regularly on Niteflirt might not have the time or privacy to splurge on an hour-long call, but they'll happily eat up your audio clips or pay for a custom. This can be a two way street– someone who buys your clips and subscribes to your fansite might splurge on a more expensive real-time session on special occasions, or when the tax refund hits.

Identify all of the sources of income you can possibly have, online and off. Identify whether they are active or passive. Is there something you already do that can become a source of income?

PRO TIP

Use all parts of the buffalo! Filming a POV video? Take stills and use them as social media fodder. Separate the audio and add it as a goodie on phone or cam sites. List the stockings you wore in the clip for sale as a bundle or an add-on.

CLIP STORES

Contributed by Oran Julius

Clip stores are a great way to earn money. Whether it is your primary method of work or something to supplement in person work, there's a way to make it useful for you. There are a variety of clip stores out there, and while most follow a similar format, there are variations. This mostly shows up regarding ToS, aka what is and is not allowed on each site. Sophie Ladder created this incredible resource which breaks down what, currently, is and isn't allowed and where: **https://bit.ly/clipsitesBDBC**

An obvious benefit to getting involved in clip stores is extra cash, but there are other greats perks to doing clip sales, including:

Space to practice skills even when you don't have clients.

Adding to brand recognition and building your reputation.

A place to highlight your niches!

Advertising for your in-person services.

Passive income… once you get them set up.

Extending your reach… get to those pockets in other places!

Getting started with clip stores takes some patience and time, because each clip needs to be done one at a time. However, once your videos are up, you don't have to do much else to sell them. Most people who use these sites are paying customers, so it's a better pool than places like Instagram or Twitter, where most people are looking for freebies. And once your clips are set to sell, they just stay there, and can generate passive income for you.

A note of caution about expectations: rarely will anyone make significant money doing clip sales alone, unless they are very prolific in creating content. This isn't said to discourage you, and I do truly believe there are benefits to having a presence on clip sites, but it does mean you should be mindful of how much time and energy you put into these efforts depending on what outcome you are hoping for.

When getting started, choose just 1-2 sites to set up. You can always add more once you have your processes down, but it's better to have many clips on one site than to have profiles on many sites with only a couple of clips.

GETTING SET UP ON A CLIP SITE

1. Choose a clip site where you would like to sell content, and apply to be a seller.

    a. You will need to submit identification proving you are of age. There is always risk in this re: internet safety & security, but you cannot sell on a formal clip site without submitting verification.

2. Use the time waiting for approval to check out other sellers who seem similar to you in terms of appearance, identities, fetishes offered, etc. If you have a lot of similarities, you'll probably be pulling from similar client bases, so observe what they are doing well and what you can learn from them.

3. Once approved, build out your profile to the specifications on the site. Pick a profile photo that advertises what buyers are getting and write a brief but intriguing description/bio.

4. Choose at least FIVE clips to start selling. Do not start advertising your profile until you have five clips up and ready to be purchased. You want buyers to have options and a reason to come back.

5. Upload each film to the site. Depending on the site, the requirements for getting the video published may vary, but most require a title, description, tags, a preview, a

still image, and the film itself. ManyVids and iWantClips (my preferred clip sites) both have ways to create a preview directly through their sites, so you don't have to make a whole trailer for your film if you don't want to (I'd say don't bother unless it's a lengthy film).

6. Advertise on the site and on social media! Utilize the social media AI settings built into most clip sites that will auto-post to your social media whenever you make a sale or upload something new (Twitter ONLY, so you don't get booted from IG).

Once you're all set up and in the habit of uploading, this will become second nature, but until you're used to it, it can be hard to remember all of the steps. Use this checklist to keep track of what you need to do for each clip from start to finish.

- ☐ Film the content
- ☐ Chop up the footage into usable clips, merge clips as needed
- ☐ Come up with a title
- ☐ Write a brief description that makes buyers curious
- ☐ Upload film to clip site
- ☐ Add title, description, and still image if required
- ☐ Choose tags that will lead the right fetishists to your clip
- ☐ Create a preview through the site or upload a readymade one
- ☐ Set your price
- ☐ Publish
- ☐ Advertise!

TIPS TO KEEP IN MIND

Shorter and cheaper clips tend to do better, so either film brief scenes or chop up longer ones into different clips.

Don't bother getting too complicated with editing. Clip sites are dominated by quick and dirty jerk-off material, not quality porn films. Just make sure you cut out any goofs, bad angles, camera drops, etc. so it doesn't look totally unprofessional. iMovie, Quicktime Player, and Davinci Resolve are all free software you can use to do these simple edits. (Davinci Resolve has much more complex capabilities as well, so maybe don't start here as it can be daunting)

WHAT IF I DON'T WANT TO DO ALL THIS, BUT REALLY WANT TO GET ON SOME CLIP SITES?

Start utilizing trade methods! Sex workers have long relied on shared skills and trading labor for each other. Many people find it easy to film clips, but difficult or tedious to do the uploading, naming, etc. process to get them ready for sale.

Do you have a friend who is in a similar boat who you can trade off with? Some people find it easier to gush about their friends than themself, so you could do the post-production labor for a friend, while they do yours.

You can also switch off taking turns with folks you shoot content with if you're not filming solos. For example, if you shoot content for two clips, each of you can take on the labor for one and send the other the write up so it's a simple copy-paste effort.

Be cautious about relying on subs to help with these tasks unless you have deep trust. They don't deserve your content for free! You can still use their help with writing descriptions/social media posts, but I strongly caution against giving them copies of footage.

Finally, if you don't have the time, energy or desire to do the labor to set up clip sales, you could hire someone to do it for you. Many sex workers are looking for part-time gigs, and this could be a way to put money back into your community if you are able.

IN SUMMARY

You don't have to do everything at once. Like Oran said, focus on one or two places in the beginning. Build systems that feel good and sustainable for you. Build systems that can support you in the event you can't do real-time sessions with clients or want to take a step back.

CHAPTER 18: CASH FLOW POST SESSION

Diversifying your income means having a leg to stand on when another one breaks. While you don't have to build them on now, have an idea for what you need in the future.

DO I HAVE A BOTTOM LINE I NEED TO MEET EACH MONTH?

HOW DO MY SESSIONS FACTOR INTO THIS MODEL?

WHAT OTHER SOURCES OF INCOME ARE AVAILABLE TO ME?

WHICH OF MY PLANNED INCOME IS PASSIVE VS ACTIVE?

HOMEWORK

Create a gift list on a wish list site.

What are some non-kinky items you can list that show your personality?

CHAPTER 19
FINANCES & INFRASTRUCTURE

Contributed by Empress Wu

Let's not lie to ourselves— part of the reason you're in this profession is that you want to make money, and you want to do it on your own terms. So let's get you set up for that.

What does financial freedom look like to you?

Maybe it looks like paying off student loans. Maybe it looks like being able to buy your mom a house, or to take care of an ailing family member. Maybe you just really really really like treating yourself. Or perhaps it's all of the above.

Doing activism/organizing work is really important, but it doesn't pay the bills! This work can create more time and space for community organizing.

Whatever the reason, let's take a minute to look at what that is for you.

What does your dream life look like?

We spend so much of our time and energy building out fantasy worlds for other people; it's time for you to do that for you.

Getting *really* clear on that is going to help you determine what kind of lifestyle you want to live.

FINANCE 101

Right now, like right this very minute, make a list of your non-negotiable monthly living costs. Rent, utilities, groceries, transportation, any debt that needs to be paid off, and any necessary medical services. Tack on 20% for savings (multiply by 1.2). This is your Freedom Fund. Divide this number by your rate, and you will know how many hours of sessions needed to make this amount.

After you have 3-6 months of Freedom Fund tucked away in a place you can't easily access, focus on paying down your debt, starting with whatever debt has the highest interest rate.

Something that changed my perspective on making money was during a conversation with Christa Daring: shift your thinking from "money that you already have" towards "how much you need to raise".

Remember: **CASH IS FLUID.** Sometimes you will have to spend money, other times, you will make more money. Money is just a means of transfer, and the number one way of having power over your finances is to TRUST that it's always going to come if you put in the work. A scarcity mentality is a self-fulfilling prophecy that will make you poorer than anything else. Living in abundance is crucial!

Bad bitches always know their net worth too, so TRACK YOUR EARNINGS AND TRACK YOUR SPENDING. BE DILIGENT ABOUT IT.

It might be scary to look at if you've never done this before, but tracking your money is the first step to being in control of it. It's easy to find expense worksheets on google, and then adjust them to fill your needs.

PRO TIP

Regardless of whether you have an LLC or a sole proprietorship, it is a good practice to separate your business and personal spending into two different accounts, especially by two different banks. Not only does it make it easier to keep track of your business spending versus personal needs spending, but it also helps protect your personal savings from being shut down.

TAXES AND INCORPORATION

[Please note: I am not an accountant and I live in the United States. These tax notes are region specific! Consult your local sex work-friendly accountant for the most accurate info]

Remember— ALL INCOME THAT COMES IN DIGITALLY SOMEWHERE IS TRACEABLE AND NEEDS TO BE REPORTED.

This includes Venmo or CashApp, even if your client just writes "gift."

You will need to be prepared to pay 20-30% in taxes on all your income, so make sure you're putting money aside to pay for it. Many companies pay taxes once every 3 months, but it's fine if you pay it all in one lump sum during tax season (it just stings a little more).

My accountant always says that your taxes should tell a story. Since you've made that long term plan up top, you need to figure out how you're going to claim shit on your taxes.

First: figure out what job title would be easiest to justify on your taxes. Buy a lot of props? Theatre consultant. Spend a lot on filming equipment? Independent film company. Have a background in the arts and can bullshit the justifications? Performance artist.

Deductions are your friend, because you can pay less in income tax, and you can deduct WAY more than you think (like your phone bill, or a portion of your apartment if you use it for only work). But remember to think long term— if you're thinking about renting a more expensive apartment, you're going to need to be able to prove you make 40x the rent annually. Even worse: want to buy a house in the next few years? You're going to need 2-3 years worth of tax returns to get approved for a mortgage.

SOLE PROPRIETORSHIP VS LLC (LIMITED LIABILITY COMPANY)

When you first enter the workforce as a business, you will be seen by the IRS as a sole proprietor, which is an unincorporated business owned and run by one person (you). You pay self-employment taxes, and in the eyes of the IRS, you and your business are one and the same. It's the simplest structure.

An LLC, on the other hand, is a legal business entity that provides limited liability protection, meaning that the owner(s) of the company are protected from the business's debts. The government now sees your company as a separate entity from you and taxes it accordingly.

You might want to open an LLC if….

- ★ You want to open a business bank account to protect your legal name
- ★ You want to protect your personal savings from the potential financial liabilities of your business
- ★ You want the tax benefits of a corporation
- ★ You want to open a business with a friend or hire someone to help you with your business

Talk to your accountant to see which one is right for you!

Keep track of every single thing that happens to you in this industry in terms of your finances. It's going to help you make more money and it's going to help you stay organized and it's going to help you see what works for you.

**FROM CAREER LONGEVITY & PROFESSIONALISM
WITH MICHELLE LACY (VOLUME III)**

MONEY TALKS

AN HONEST CONVERSATION ABOUT RATES

Money can be pretty emotional. But the stories we tell ourselves about money are often bullshit. Society at large tells us that the better we are at our jobs, the more money we will make, which is patently untrue. There are folks who are VERY GOOD at their jobs who are grinding away for peanuts, and folks who are basically failing upwards.

Only you can set your rates, but this can be complicated for many reasons. If everyone in your area is charging $500/hour, will you be seen as undercutting or less than for charging $400? If your area is filled with $200/hour but you can't leave the house for less than $350, do you feel like you have to justify this rate gap to your clients? Do you have a standard rate for every client or does it change based on the person?

What you charge should feel good to you. We all want more money, but in an ideal world, the cash you walk out with after seeing a client should make you feel content and secure. We like to say: if someone is paying it, it's a good rate. Hourly rates often feel deeply personal, but a higher rate does not equate to a better provider.

PRO TIP

This one sounds woo-woo, but is a tried and true strip club trick: If you have a great day of sessions (online or off) stick around for an extra hour and funnel that into your business. Whether that's being available on the phone, cam, or queuing up marketing materials for social media. The confidence of someone who's just made a bunch of money doing what they love shines through.

Rates often correlate heavily with boundaries. Rent is due, so you might be tempted to take that session with the client who asks for a discount. That's a decision only you can make. You might be inclined to put up with a boundary crosser or an emotionally exhausting client because they're a big spender. Remember that this money comes at a price. Burnout is real and it happens to the best of us.

When you determine your rates for various things, consider the market. Your area, your offerings, and your experience level will all factor into your decision. It's tempting to price at the high end, but it's better to be booked and steady than it is to wait on that one $1k client to roll through.

SO HOW MUCH DO I ACTUALLY CHARGE?

Figure out what your base rate is for a standard session, whatever that means to you. This should be a rate that you feel good about regardless of if you make anything on top of it. Some charge more for certain types of sessions, i.e. ones with extensive prep, sessions involving extra fluids, more erotic sessions, or things they hate. With the abundance of menus online, it may be tempting to charge a separate fee for each individual kink or several add ons. Don't get caught up in nickel-and-diming your client. Understanding your sessions boundaries and interests will inform what you should and shouldn't charge more for. We obviously all want more money, but we shouldn't have to use a calculator or pricing matrix graph to figure out exactly how much a session will cost.

Don't let money define your worth. This is easier said than done, but you are not worth less (or more) because your rates are lower (or higher) than others.

> ## IN SUMMARY
>
> Set up your finances with intention. Watch them like you watch your clients. Money can be emotional and in SW it sometimes feels even heavier, like you worked too hard for every dollar. Whether you're full-time or doing this as a side gig, dominating your finances is easy when you come at it with a clear head. Don't take the numbers on the sheet as a value of your physical or emotional worth.

CHAPTER 19: FINANCES & INFRASTRUCTURE

We all want to make money, but how do you keep track of it?
How will your rates change and when?

HOW WILL I DECIDE MY INITIAL RATE?

WILL MY RATE BE THE SAME ACROSS ALL CLIENTS?

DOES MY RATE CHANGE BASED ON HOW MANY HOURS ARE BOOKED?

WHAT WILL I TRACK IN REGARDS TO FINANCES? BY INCOME SOURCE? BY CLIENT? HOW OFTEN?

WHAT IS MY IDEAL BOOKING - # OF HOURS AND $$?	**WHAT SERVICES OR ACTIVITIES WILL I CHARGE MORE FOR, IF AT ALL?**
WHEN WILL I CHOOSE TO COMMUNICATE MY RATE TO CLIENTS?	**HOW WILL I KNOW WHEN IT IS TIME TO RAISE MY RATES?**

CASE STUDIES

Keep in mind in many cases when we look at successful Dominants, they have already worked through the toughest bits to get where they are. We are seeing the finished product.

Eva Oh is a high-end Domme, which you can see from her marketing alone. She's only accessible to the few capable to serve her– and that's the point. Eva has carefully grown her brand over many years so she can be picky about who she sees, and only take days-long client excursions. Her most famous work, youwillpleaseme.com, gamifies domination while allowing her wannabe submissives experience serving her without ever directly interacting with them.

Neena De Ville, like many Dominants, utilizes blog posts on her website. At a baseline, blog posts will help with SEO because you're including more of the words that could be pulled from search engines when your potential clients are keyboard jockeying. Taking it a step further, Neena's blogs assist in her protocol, eliminating the need for further email back and forth.

Troy Orleans famously said "I've seen too many dicks," meaning she has paid her dues by taking all sorts of sessions to pay the bills and get by. Now she is in a position of choice. Troy has made a name for herself as THE heavy bondage dominant. The focus of her sessions and her niche outweigh the traditional idea of branding. Troy doesn't show her face in marketing or media appearances. You won't find her in leather and latex, but rather leggings.

Veda X's style is very low protocol and casual. They do not use an honorific. They talk like a frat bro. They are openly disgusting and do lots of work with scent play. Their clientele tends to skew younger. Veda operates on in person sessions only. No content, no fan site. Veda gets very consistent bookings.

Lola Jean's primary income is sex education, and sex work is her side hustle. Her sex ed fans are unhinged, so she doesn't advertise or mention it on her social media, but you know she offers sessions. Lola does not use advertising sites or listings on traditional domination sites, exclusively using wrestling sites. Potential clients have to go through wrestling channels to reach her.

Shayla Lange gets a large majority of her clients through Twitter, where she shitposts and generally shoots the shit with other Dominants. 50% of her income comes from running a dungeon, which has allowed her to dump clients she hates and spend more time with ones who inspire her. Rarely does she advertise to "potential clients"– they contact Shayla as a byproduct through her relationships with others in the industry. Her relationships and reputation do the heavy lifting.

BABY DOM/ME/MX BOOTCAMP WRAP-UP

We know it can be very exciting and overwhelming, but your career won't be built in a day. Parse out bite sized pieces to make starting your new vocation or side hustle more manageable.

WHAT IS MY DOM/ME/MX PERSONA?

WHAT IS A MARKER OF SUCCESS FOR ME?

HOW DO I WANT MY PRACTICE TO LOOK? HOW DO I MANAGE THIS?

WHAT IS MY SELLING POINT? WHAT MAKES ME DIFFERENT?	WHO IS MY IDEAL CLIENT AND HOW WILL I SPEAK TO THEM?

HOW WILL I ENGAGE AND DEVELOP RELATIONSHIPS WITHIN THE COMMUNITY?

WHAT ARE 3 THINGS I CAN DO OR IMPLEMENT THIS WEEK?

DESCRIBE YOUR IDEAL CLIENT WITHOUT USING WORDS RELATED TO MONEY.

RESOURCES & DISCOUNT CODES

7 Days of Domination
Use code SWISWORK for 70% off all full-week series and bundles.
Lovelorn Lingerie (harnesses & leather)
use code EVERYDAMNDAY20 for 20% off

RECOMMENDED READING

- ★ Lola Davina - *Thriving in Sex Work*
- ★ Peggy Orenstein - *Boys & Sex*
- ★ Amberley Rothfield - *90 Days and Paid*
- ★ Princess Kali - *Authentic Kink*
- ★ Tina Horn - *Why Are People Into That? A Cultural Investigation of Kink*
- ★ Jiz Lee - *Coming Out Like a Porn Star*
- ★ Dossie Easton & Janet W. Hardy - *The New Topping Book*
- ★ Melissa Gira Grant - *Playing the Whore*
- ★ Juno Mac & Molly Smith - *Revolting Prostitutes*
- ★ Shay Tiziano & Stefanos Tiziano - *Creating Captivating Classes*
- ★ Princess Kali - *365 Days of Kink*
- ★ Virginie Despenstes & Frank Wynee - *King Kong Theory*
- ★ Ariane Cruz - *The Color of Kink*
- ★ Nickie Roberts - *Whores in History*
- ★ Cyndi Suarez - *The Power Manual: How to Master Complex Power Dynamics*

STILL WANT TO LEARN MORE?

Baby Dom/me/mx Bootcamp started as an in person bootcamp, because of the intangibles that can only be gathered face to face, the immediate built-in community with fellow boot campers, as well as private one-on-one time with the headmistresses and our featured presenters.

While this workbook provides the self-study you need to catapult your new career or side hustle, we do know that sometimes education and community is best built in person. Baby Dom/me/mx Bootcamp tours in multiple cities throughout the world including, but not limited to, NYC, Los Angeles, London, Houston and more...

Interested in having Baby Dom/me/mx Bootcamp near you? Send us an email, note, or DM of where you'd like to see us pop up next.

ABOUT THE AUTHORS

7 DAYS OF DOMINATION creates accessible on-demand kink education from a harm reduction lens that centers community, while closing the gap of traditionally gatekept training. In addition to their keystone Baby Dom/me/mx Bootcamp, 7 Days of Domination features an ever-growing library of kink education from Pros all over the world.

LOLA JEAN (she/they) is a sex educator, fetish wrestler, and the world record holder in volume squirting. Lola provides no-frills sex education through a variety of mediums to help us question our belief patterns and free individuals through cycles of shame to find their own autonomy. She can be found at @lolajeandotcom.

SHAYLA LANGE (she/her) is a Pro-Domme, educator, and owner of NYC's largest female-owned dungeon. A sex worker of 15+ years, she believes in a harm-reduction focused approach to the world's oldest profession. Mistress Shayla loves long walks on the beach and hitting men with sticks. She can be found at @YesMissShayla.

CONTRIBUTORS

EMPRESS WU (she/her) is an Asian-American professional dominatrix based in NYC who specializes in breathplay, edgeplay, and psychological BDSM scenes. Empress Wu became a professional dominatrix after being held up at gunpoint at the age of 18. Since then, She has been obsessed with fear, how it can be constructed, how it can be destroyed, and how it can be used as a tool for healing both environmental and inherited trauma. You can find her at empresswu.net

ORAN JULIUS (they/he) is a femmeboy himbo, multitasking maven, and creative dreamer. Oran is a thick, Black, queer, nonbinary, neurodivergent and disabled human. He is a vers, queer slut and a true switch who loves to play with extremes, swinging from unsettling sadism to eager masochism. A role play enthusiast who embraces the term Mommy, they lean into the taboo and depraved. Oran is the founder of ColorBlock Films, an independent ethical porn studio based in NYC, designed to celebrate and center humans not often featured in porn. You can find them at @juicyfruitoran

MIA DARQUE (she/her) is a Giantess, gamer, and sadistic nerd with a femdom superiority complex. Also known as the Oklahoma Amazon, Mia has been practicing BDSM for 20+ years specializing in ABDL, extreme corporal punishments, lift & carry, and interrogations, with a soft spot for nerdcore roleplays, because, duh. You can find her at justsayred.com

ACKNOWLEDGEMENTS

There are so many people to thank that assisted in writing this book. We've come a long way from the initial version of this book, which was just a set of homework questions, to the second edition which we literally wrote on an airplane.

First and foremost, we would like to thank the whores who came before us and, of course, the whores who come after us.

We would like to thank the New York Delegation for loving us, supporting us, and calling us out on our bullshit when we needed it most.

To our editor - thank you for suffering with us from day one. Thank you for suffering an additional time by editing this book.

Princess Kali for having faith in us. For your friendship, inspiration, validation and your extremely cool convention 'fits.

Thank you to the 7DOD fam and to anyone who has ever taught a class for 7 Days of Domination. We are nothing without you.

Thank you to our civilian friends for keeping us humble and grounded and not flinching when we talk about stabbing people.

Thank you to the countless number of workers who recommend our work to newbies.

Thank you to Veda for being the best first employee we could ever ask for. You are the future of 7 Days of Domination and we can't wait to see how you grow.

Thank you to all of the alumni who have taken our Bootcamp in person. We continue to learn and grow from you. We can teach all day long, but y'all did the work and we're so proud of each and every one of you.

Thank you to anyone who has ever taken a 7DOD class, liked a social media post, bought a Chaos Gremlin hat, or came to any of our events. Your support means the world to us.

And finally, this book is dedicated to anyone who has ever learned the hard way to say no, or realized it's not that easy to sell feet pics online.

7D·D KINK FEELINGS CHART

SELECT AS MANY FEELINGS THAT CONVEY HOW YOU WANT TO FEEL DURING AND/OR AFTER PLAY

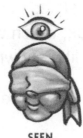 SEEN

 PLAYFUL

 OBJECTIFIED

 ENRAPTURED

 USEFUL

 CHALLENGED

 OVERWHELMED

 HONORED

 DIRTY

 NERVOUS

 EMPOWERED

 ADORED

 DEGRADED

 SMALL

 USED

WWW.7DAYSOFDOMINATION.COM

© MEG DANIELS, 2022

Made in the USA
Middletown, DE
23 June 2024

56006769R00099